50 EASY INDIAN CURRIES

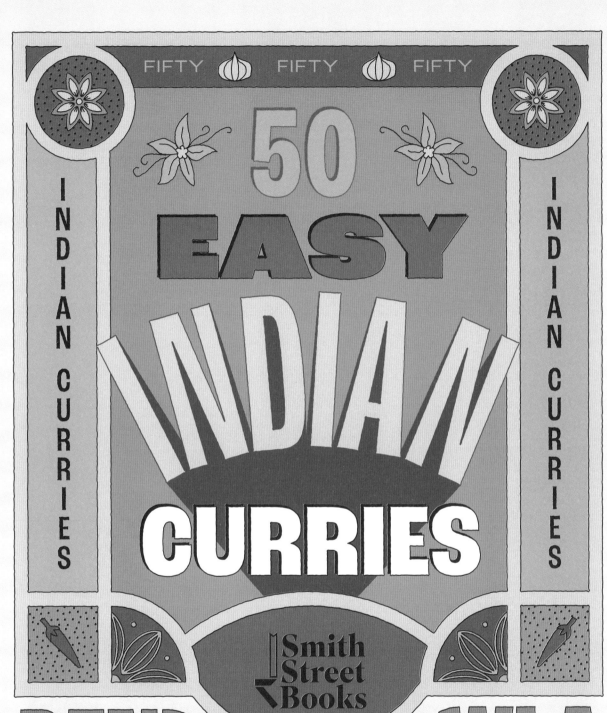

FIFTY · FIFTY · FIFTY

50
EASY
INDIAN
CURRIES

INDIAN CURRIES

INDIAN CURRIES

Smith
Street
Books

PENNY CHAWLA

Introduction
6

The Indian Pantry
8

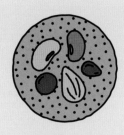

11

Pulses & Legumes

25

Vegetables

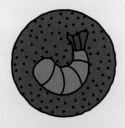

53

Seafood

69

Chicken

89

Pork & Beef

103

Lamb

123

Basics

Index
134

Introduction

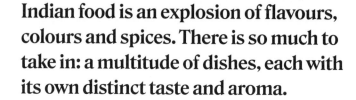

Indian food is an explosion of flavours, colours and spices. There is so much to take in: a multitude of dishes, each with its own distinct taste and aroma.

If you're new to cooking Indian curries at home, you might feel a little overwhelmed. But once you stop to take it all in and begin to delve into the different recipes the country of India has to offer, things will start to fall into place. Armed with this book, your journey into Indian cuisine will be easy to understand and enjoyable, and change any preconceived ideas that Indian food is difficult to cook.

With 29 states and seven union territories, it is said that the language and food of India changes every 100 km (60 miles) as you travel the subcontinent. Every state has its own regional specialties, and then there are sub-cuisines depending on religion, caste, the climate and availability of local ingredients. For example, a lentil stew called sambar, known throughout the southern states, will be made slightly differently wherever you visit. And, unsurprisingly, everyone claims that their version is the best.

It would be impossible to put all the curries of India in a single book. Great tomes have been written, and still none can be considered truly comprehensive – such is the nature of a cuisine that caters for almost 1.4 billion people and where the ingredients used in a dish can change from village to village and even household to household, all without recipes to guide them. It is testament to Indians' love of food that a recipe will be refined and perfected over time to suit personal tastes: a little more spice here; a different vegetable there, and then passed down through the generations to create family favourites.

Despite these subtle differences, there are of course popular dishes that everyone cooks and for which India is famous, and here we have collected 50 of the best (and easiest) curries to make from scratch. From restaurant classics, such as butter chicken, dal makhani, pork vindaloo and saag paneer, to lesser-known regional gems including beef Madras, Bengali fish curry and the delightful papad ki sabzi, where papadams are added into the curry sauce for unctuous results, there is a curry here for everyone. In addition, you will find simple recipes for pastes, rice and breads to complete your Indian meal.

With a few essential Indian pantry staples and fresh ingredients, all of which can be found at any supermarket, each curry can be made in an hour or less, or thrown into a saucepan and left to slow cook on the stove while you get on with something else. If you're already a seasoned curry cook, then enjoy these simplified favourites or try out some of the regional specialties that you may not have come across before.

It goes without saying that vegans and vegetarians are well catered for when it comes to Indian cuisine and the recipes here are no exception. With dals aplenty and a wide range of flavourful vegetable dishes, a meat-free banquet is easy to create. Paneer, the beloved Indian cheese, can be easily swapped for tofu, while yoghurt can be substituted for coconut yoghurt for even more plant-based options.

So get ready to start your Indian curry adventure. Find your favourites and learn how to cook them with ease. Serve several curries together with your choice of rice, pilau and breads to create your own Indian feast, or whip up a simple dal for a nourishing midweek meal. Once you gain confidence, you'll find yourself adding your own twists and flourishes, and soon these curries will become your very own.

The Indian Pantry

Here are some of the common ingredients you will find in every Indian pantry. Stock up on the below and you'll always be ready to make your favourite curry.

Turmeric

Indigenous to India, Indian kitchens would be colourless without this wonderful spice. Known not just for its culinary use but also for medicinal and antiseptic qualities, turmeric is also the only spice that Hindus use for devotional purposes. The active ingredient in turmeric is curcumin, which is known for its healing properties.

Chillies

Indian food is almost incomplete without chillies yet, ironically, the chilli plant is foreign to India, arriving with the Portuguese in the 15th century. Indian cuisine uses green and red fresh chillies, along with chilli powder, the most famous of which comes from Kashmir.

Garam Masala

A spice blend that roughly translates to 'hot spice', but actually doesn't contain much heat. It is made by dry-roasting different types and quantities of spices and then blending them together. Garam masala is typically added at the end of cooking, the purpose being to add aroma and flavour, without overpowering the final dish.

Cloves

Part of the myrtle family, the name clove comes from the Latin word 'clavus', which means nail. Cloves are not native to India, but they are grown in small quantities in Kerala. They have a strong, astringent flavour profile, and should be used sparingly in dishes.

Cardamom

A spice that grows abundantly in the beautiful state of Kerala due to its tropical climate. From teas to spice mixes, meat-based curries and desserts, cardamom is a perfumed spice that is much loved throughout India. The recipes in this book use both green and black cardamom pods.

Asafoetida

Pure asafoetida or 'heeng', has a strong, almost off-putting smell that dissipates when cooked. It is used as a substitute for garlic and onions by Indians who avoid these ingredients, and just a pinch of asafoetida is enough to flavour a dish. You will find it in any Indian grocery store, sold in small plastic containers, diluted with rice or wheat flour to dull down the pungent smell. Apart from adding flavour to food, it is also a very good digestive.

Fenugreek

Little is known of how this spice reached India; however, it is a popular staple in the Indian pantry. The whole seeds are used as a tempering in dals, as well as being added to Indian pickles. Fresh fenugreek leaves are used extensively in cooking and their dried form, known as 'kasuri methi', is sprinkled on top of cooked dishes for its aromatic quality. A true wonder spice.

Coriander

Coriander seeds are used extensively in Indian cuisine for their warm, nutty flavour profile. Lightly toasted, they become even more fragrant and, when powdered, they tone down other strong flavours, such as chilli. Coriander (cilantro) leaves are always added as a garnish, and never cooked, to retain their vibrant green colour.

Cinnamon

Unlike the West, where cinnamon is often reserved for baking, in India it is part of a collection of whole spices that are added to curries. Often confused with cassia, which comes from China and has a slight amount of heat, real cinnamon only grows in Sri Lanka. Cinnamon is aromatic and adds a deep flavour to dishes.

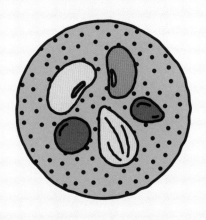

Pulses &
Legumes

Dal Makhani

The quintessential Indian dal found in every Indian restaurant all over the world is also one of the easiest to make. Dal makhani means buttered dal, not because it is cooked in a lot of butter, but because the lentils used to make this dal have a soft buttery texture when slow-cooked. Once you master this dish, you will return to it often, especially when you crave comfort.

100 g (3½ oz) urad dal (black gram), well rinsed
100 g (3½ oz) dried red kidney beans, well rinsed
60 g (¼ cup) chana dal (split chickpeas/yellow split peas), well rinsed
1 cinnamon stick
5 green cardamom pods, bruised
5 cloves
400 g (14 oz) tin crushed tomatoes
100 g (3½ oz) unsalted butter, chopped
2 tablespoons ginger and garlic paste
1 tablespoon chilli powder, or to taste
¼ teaspoon ground turmeric
sea salt
1 tablespoon dried fenugreek leaves, crushed
Steamed basmati rice (see page 124) and papadams, to serve

Place the urad dal, kidney beans and chana dal in a large bowl and cover generously with water. Cover and set aside to soak overnight.

Place the cinnamon stick, cardamom and cloves in a square of muslin (cheesecloth), then gather into a bundle and secure with kitchen string.

The next day, drain the dal mixture and transfer to a large saucepan, along with 750 ml (3 cups) of water and the spice bundle. Bring to the boil over high heat, skimming off any froth that rises to the surface. Reduce the heat to low and simmer, stirring occasionally, for about 1½ hours, until the dal is tender. Add a little more boiling water if the mixture starts to stick to the bottom of the pan or is becoming too thick.

Remove and discard the spice bundle. Add the tomatoes, butter, ginger and garlic paste, chilli powder, turmeric and a good pinch of salt. Increase the heat to medium and cook, stirring frequently, for 10 minutes. The consistency should be like a thick soup. Taste, and adjust the seasoning if necessary. Stir in the fenugreek leaves.

Serve with steamed basmati rice and papadams on the side.

Dal Tadka

Every city in India has their own version of dal tadka. A simple change of spice, or the ingredients used in the temper and, voila, you can have a different dal every single day. The key to this dish is the tadka, a flavoured oil of sorts that's infused with spices and brings out the flavour of any dal you make. You can make the dal in advance and cook the tadka just before serving.

1 tablespoon ghee
1 onion, chopped
2 teaspoons ginger and garlic paste
½ teaspoon ground turmeric
1 teaspoon ground coriander
250 g (1 cup) masoor dal
   (split red lentils), well rinsed
sea salt
Steamed basmati rice
   (see page 124), to serve
natural yoghurt, to serve

Tadka
3 tablespoons ghee
½ teaspoon black mustard seeds
½ teaspoon cumin seeds
1 sprig curry leaves
2 small dried red chillies
2 garlic cloves, sliced
pinch of asafoetida
½ teaspoon chilli powder

Heat the ghee in a large heavy-based saucepan over medium–low heat and add the onion and ginger and garlic paste. Cook, stirring occasionally, for 5–6 minutes, until the onion is tender and starting to colour. Stir in the turmeric and coriander and cook for 1 minute or until fragrant. Add the masoor dal and 750 ml (3 cups) of water.

Increase the heat to medium and bring to the boil, then reduce the heat to low and simmer, stirring occasionally, for 25–30 minutes, until the lentils are soft and broken down. Add a little more boiling water if the mixture starts to stick to the base of the pan or is becoming too thick. Season with salt to taste.

To make the tadka, heat the ghee in a frying pan over medium heat. Add the mustard seeds, cumin and curry leaves and sizzle for a few seconds, then add the dried chillies, garlic and asafoetida and cook, stirring occasionally, for 1–2 minutes, until the garlic is golden. Remove from the heat and stir in the chilli powder.

Pour the dal into a serving dish and pour the hot tadka over the top. Serve with steamed basmati rice and natural yoghurt or as an accompaniment to any Indian meal.

Chana Masala

Chana, or chickpeas, are an important protein for vegetarians and a huge part of the North Indian diet, where they're eaten for breakfast, lunch or dinner. Packed with flavour and simple to make, you can never go wrong with a bowl of nourishing chana dal.

2 tablespoons ghee or peanut oil
1 teaspoon cumin seeds
1 onion, chopped
1 tablespoon ginger and
    garlic paste
1 bird's eye chilli, finely chopped
1½ teaspoons sweet paprika
1 teaspoon ground coriander
¼ teaspoon ground turmeric
2 large tomatoes, finely chopped
800 g (1 lb 12 oz) tinned chickpeas
    (garbanzo beans), drained
1 teaspoon garam masala
freshly squeezed lemon juice,
    to taste

To serve
coriander (cilantro) leaves (optional)
Steamed basmati rice
    (see page 124)
lemon wedges

Heat the ghee or oil in a saucepan over medium heat. Add the cumin seeds and allow to sizzle for 10 seconds, then add the onion and cook, stirring occasionally, for 5–6 minutes, until starting to brown. Add the ginger and garlic paste and chilli and cook for 1 minute or until fragrant. Add the paprika, coriander and turmeric and cook, stirring, for 2 minutes or until fragrant. Add the tomato and stir for 1 minute, then add 250 ml (1 cup) of water and a good pinch of salt. Bring to the boil, cover, then reduce the heat and simmer for 10 minutes for the flavours to develop.

Add the chickpeas, then bring to the boil again. Reduce the heat, cover and simmer, stirring occasionally, for 20 minutes. Remove the lid and simmer for a further 10–15 minutes, until the sauce is thickened and the spices have mellowed. Add a little more boiling water if the mixture starts to stick to the base of the pan or is becoming too thick. Remove from the heat and stir in the garam masala and lemon juice to taste. Taste and adjust the seasoning if necessary.

Serve topped with a few coriander leaves, if desired, and with steamed basmati rice and lemon wedges on the side.

Moong Dal

Moong dal is a staple in every Indian home, and will be made differently depending on which part of India you are in. If you're feeling under the weather, you can't go wrong with a bowl of moong dal, as it's easy to digest and very nutritious. According to traditional Indian Ayurvedic medicine, it also balances the body's elements.

210 g (1 cup) moong dal (skinned split mung beans), well rinsed
¼ teaspoon ground turmeric
sea salt
Steamed basmati rice (see page 124) or Paratha (see page 128), to serve

Moong dal temper
2 tablespoons ghee or peanut oil
1–2 dried red chillies
½ teaspoon cumin seeds
½ teaspoon fenugreek seeds
⅛ teaspoon asafoetida
1 Asian shallot, thinly sliced
1 sprig curry leaves, leaves stripped

Place the moong dal in a saucepan and add 800 ml (27 fl oz) of water. Bring to the boil over high heat and skim off the froth that rises to the surface. Stir in the turmeric, then reduce the heat to medium–low, cover, leaving the lid open a crack, and simmer, stirring occasionally, for 35–40 minutes, until the moong dal is soft and broken down. Add a little more boiling water if the mixture starts to stick to the base of the pan or is becoming too thick. Add salt to taste. Remove from the heat and set aside.

To make the moong dal temper, heat the ghee or oil in a heavy-based frying pan over medium–high heat. Add the chilli, cumin seeds, fenugreek seeds and asafoetida. Shake the pan for about 30 seconds and as soon as the chillies start to darken add the shallot and curry leaves. Cook, stirring, for 2–3 minutes, until the shallot starts to brown.

Give the dal a stir and thin with a little boiling water if necessary. Pour into a serving dish, top with the temper and stir until just combined.

Serve with steamed basmati rice or paratha.

Chana Dal

Chana dal or Bengal gram (also known as split chickpeas) are delightfully nutty and earthy in taste. Unlike other lentils, chana dal need to be cooked al dente, so they have a slight bite. They can be cooked in a variety of ways and added to soups, salads and even desserts.

220 g (1 cup) chana dal (split chickpeas/yellow split peas), well rinsed
1½ teaspoons ground turmeric
½ teaspoon ground cardamom
1 fresh or dried bay leaf
sea salt
½ teaspoon garam masala
freshly squeezed lemon juice, to taste
Simple naan (see page 126), to serve

Chana dal temper
2 tablespoons ghee or sunflower oil
6 cloves
½ teaspoon black mustard seeds
2 dried red chillies, cracked open
pinch of asafoetida
4 garlic cloves, crushed
½ teaspoon cumin seeds

Combine the chana dal, turmeric, cardamom, bay leaf and 1 litre (4 cups) of water in a large heavy-based saucepan over medium heat and bring to the boil. Reduce the heat to a low simmer, cover, leaving the lid open a crack and cook, stirring occasionally, for 50–60 minutes, until the chana dal is soft and broken down (see note). Add a little more boiling water if the mixture starts to stick to the base of the pan or is becoming too thick. Remove and discard the bay leaf and season generously with salt. Purée with a stick blender if you prefer a smoother dal.

To make the temper, heat the ghee or oil in a small saucepan over medium–high heat. Add the cloves, mustard seeds and chilli and cook, shaking the pan, until the seeds start to crackle. Add the asafoetida, garlic and cumin seeds and cook, stirring constantly, for 30 seconds or until fragrant.

Pour the temper over the dal and add the garam masala. Stir gently to combine. Taste and season with salt and a good squeeze of lemon juice.

Serve with naan bread on the side.

Note: You can reduce the cooking time of the dal by soaking the chana dal in cold water for 2–3 hours prior to cooking. Drain and follow the recipe, reducing the cooking time to about 30 minutes.

Papad Ki Sabzi

A curry can be made out of seemingly endless ingredients. How else do you explain this dish made from papadams? Papad ki sabzi is a specialty of Rajasthan, a very dry state known for the resourceful ways in which ingredients are used to make the most delicious of dishes. The papadams turn soft in the curry and almost melt in your mouth.

2 tablespoons coconut or peanut oil
½ teaspoon cumin seeds
pinch of asafoetida
1 onion, finely chopped
3 teaspoons ginger and garlic paste
2 long green chillies, split
    lengthways
1 teaspoon dried fenugreek leaves,
    crushed
1 teaspoon ground coriander
½ teaspoon chilli powder
½ teaspoon ground turmeric
250 g (1 cup) natural yoghurt
sea salt
5 large cooked papadams
handful of coriander (cilantro),
    roughly chopped
Steamed basmati rice (see
    page 124) or Chapattis
    (see page 131), to serve

Heat the oil in a saucepan over medium heat. Add the cumin seeds and sizzle for a few seconds until they crackle, then add the asafoetida. Add the onion, ginger and garlic paste, green chilli and fenugreek leaves and cook, stirring occasionally, for 8–10 minutes, until the onion is soft.

Stir through the ground spices until fragrant, then reduce the heat to low. Whisk in the yoghurt, then add 125 ml (½ cup) of water. Bring to a gentle simmer, stirring constantly, and season to taste. Break the papadams into 5 cm (2 in) pieces and add to the mixture along with the coriander and stir well.

Serve immediately with steamed basmati rice or chapattis.

Vegetables

Eggplant Masala

Eggplant is a popular ingredient in Indian cuisine. Roasted, grilled or fried, it adds a 'meatiness' to vegetarian curries. This eggplant masala is simple and quick to make and goes perfectly with other curries as part of a larger Indian banquet. The yoghurt adds a delightful fresh touch.

2 large (about 900 g/2 lb) eggplants
(aubergines), cut into 2 cm
(¾ in) chunks
½ teaspoon sea salt
2 tablespoons ghee or vegetable oil
1 teaspoon black mustard seeds
3 Asian shallots, sliced
2 cm (¾ in) piece of ginger, finely
grated
2 garlic cloves, thinly sliced
1 long red chilli, chopped
400 g (14 oz) tin crushed tomatoes
½ teaspoon ground cinnamon
¼ teaspoon ground cardamom
pinch of ground cloves
60 g (¼ cup) natural yoghurt
coriander (cilantro) leaves, to serve
papadams, to serve

Place the eggplant in a large bowl and sprinkle with the salt. Toss to combine and set aside for 30 minutes. Rinse well and pat dry with paper towel.

Heat a large heavy-based non-stick frying pan over high heat. Working in batches if necessary, add the eggplant to the dry pan and cook, stirring occasionally, for 5–6 minutes per batch, until lightly browned all over. Transfer to a plate and set aside.

Heat the ghee or oil in the same frying pan over medium–high heat. Add the mustard seeds and sizzle for a few seconds. When the seeds start to crackle, add the shallot, ginger, garlic and chilli. Reduce the heat to medium and cook for 4–5 minutes, stirring occasionally, until the onion is golden. Add the tomatoes, cinnamon, cardamom, cloves and 125 ml (½ cup) of water and return the eggplant to the pan. Cover and cook, stirring occasionally, for 10–15 minutes, until the eggplant is very tender and the sauce has thickened slightly. Season with a little salt, if necessary.

Spoon the yoghurt over the curry, scatter with coriander leaves and serve with papadams on the side.

Saag Aloo

Saag is a medley of bitter greens, such as mustard, collards and turnip, usually made during the winter months in North India. This dish uses readily available spinach, which is sweeter than the traditional greens. The crispy potatoes fried in ghee blend perfectly with the soft spinach.

3 tablespoons ghee
1 teaspoon black mustard seeds
1 onion, chopped
3 garlic cloves, thinly sliced
3 cm (1¼ in) piece of ginger, finely
    grated
1 teaspoon cumin seeds
1 teaspoon ground turmeric
½ teaspoon chilli powder
600 g (1 lb 5 oz) waxy or
    all-purpose potatoes, scrubbed
    and chopped into 1.5 cm (½ in)
    pieces
sea salt
200 g (7 oz) baby spinach leaves
squeeze of lemon juice, to taste
    (optional)

Heat 1 tablespoon of the ghee in a large non-stick frying pan over medium heat and add the mustard seeds. Let the seeds sizzle for a few seconds, until they start to crackle. Add the onion, ginger, garlic and spices and cook, stirring, for 4–5 minutes, until the onion is deep golden. Transfer to a plate with a slotted spoon.

Add the remaining ghee, the potato and a generous pinch of salt to the same frying pan. Stir to coat the potato in the ghee and add 80 ml (⅓ cup) of water. Cover, and cook for 5 minutes or until the potato starts to soften. Remove the lid and cook for a further 10–15 minutes, letting the potato cook undisturbed for periods of time so that a nice crust forms.

Return the onion mixture to the pan and add the spinach, turning gently until wilted. Season to taste and add a little lemon juice if you like.

Serve as part of a shared meal with your choice of rice, breads and other curries.

Kerala Egg Roast

The state of Kerala is known for its stunning backwaters and authentic Ayurvedic treatments. However, the food of Kerala is equally as famous. Known as 'God's own country', Keralans pride themselves in the freshness of their ingredients and their spicy, fiery curries. This egg curry is cooked in a thick sauce made with tomatoes and sweet caramelised onions.

2 tablespoons coconut or peanut oil
1 teaspoon black mustard seeds
2 onions, thinly sliced
1 tablespoon ginger and
    garlic paste
1 small green chilli, split lengthways
8 large free-range eggs, at room
    temperature
250 g (1 cup) tomato passata
    (puréed tomatoes)
2 sprigs curry leaves, leaves
    stripped
1 teaspoon chilli powder
1 teaspoon ground coriander
1 teaspoon ground turmeric
½ teaspoon ground fennel
½ teaspoon freshly ground
    black pepper
sea salt
handful of coriander (cilantro)
    leaves, roughly chopped,
    plus extra to serve
Steamed basmati rice
    (see page 124), to serve

Heat the oil in a heavy-based frying pan over medium heat. Add the mustard seeds and sizzle for a few seconds until they start to crackle. Add the onion, ginger and garlic paste and green chilli, and cook, stirring occasionally, for 5–6 minutes, until the onion is tender.

Meanwhile, gently lower the eggs into a small saucepan of boiling water. Reduce the heat to medium–low and cook for 8 minutes for eggs that are just hard-boiled (or 6 minutes for a jammy yolk). Drain and run the eggs under cold water. Gently peel when cool enough to handle.

Add the passata, curry leaves, spices and 180 ml (¾ cup) of water to the onion mixture and season with salt. Cook, stirring frequently, for 8–10 minutes, until the mixture is slightly thickened. Add the peeled eggs and coriander and gently stir to coat the eggs well.

Scatter with the extra coriander and serve with steamed basmati rice.

Sindhi Kadhi

Kadhi is a yoghurt-based sauce, and there are many varieties in India. However, sindhi kadhi is uniquely vegan as it uses a roux made with chickpea flour to replicate the creamy yoghurt. Think of it as a light, tangy vegan soup, best enjoyed with rice.

1 large potato, peeled and chopped
    into 2 cm (¾ in) pieces
100 g (3½ oz) drumstick vegetable
    or green beans, sliced
3 tablespoons vegetable oil
100 g (3½ oz) okra, halved
    lengthways
½ teaspoon cumin seeds
½ teaspoon fenugreek seeds
pinch of asafoetida
1 sprig curry leaves, leaves stripped
30 g (¼ cup) besan (chickpea flour)
1–2 small green chillies, chopped
1 cm (½ in) piece of ginger, finely
    grated
½ teaspoon Kashmiri chilli powder
¼ teaspoon ground turmeric
2 teaspoons tamarind purée, plus
    extra to taste
sea salt
Steamed basmati rice
    (see page 124), to serve

Separately boil or steam the potato and drumstick vegetable or green beans until tender. Strain, reserving the cooking water.

Heat half the oil in a large heavy-based frying pan over medium heat. Add the okra and cook, stirring occasionally, for 3–4 minutes, until lightly browned and tender, then transfer to a plate with a slotted spoon.

Add the remaining oil to the pan, along with the cumin and fenugreek seeds. When they start to crackle, add the asafoetida and curry leaves and stir well, then stir in the besan. Cook, stirring, for 1–2 minutes, until golden brown and well toasted. Add enough water to the reserved cooking water to make up 625 ml (2½ cups), then add this to the pan along with the green chilli, ginger, chilli powder and turmeric and stir well. Add the cooked vegetables and tamarind purée and bring to the boil. Reduce the heat to a simmer and cook for 2–3 minutes, for the flavours to develop. Season well with salt and more tamarind purée if desired.

Serve with steamed basmati rice.

Mushroom Matar

Mushrooms are less common in Indian cuisine, which is surprising because their meaty texture works well with spicy curries and gravies, as showcased here in this mushroom matar. To make this dish vegan, simply substitute vegetable oil for the ghee and omit the natural yoghurt.

2 tablespoons ghee
2 onions, thinly sliced
sea salt
2 teaspoons ginger and garlic paste
1 teaspoon Kashmiri chilli powder
1 teaspoon ground turmeric
½ teaspoon ground cumin
½ teaspoon ground coriander
1 long green chilli, split
250 g (1 cup) tomato passata
    (puréed tomatoes)
300 g (10½ oz) button mushrooms,
    thickly sliced
130 g (1 cup) frozen baby peas,
    thawed
1 teaspoon dried fenugreek leaves,
    crushed
½ teaspoon garam masala
Steamed basmati rice (see
    page 124) or Simple naan
    (see page 126), to serve
natural yoghurt, to serve (optional)

Heat the ghee in a large heavy-based frying pan over medium–low heat. Add the onion and ½ teaspoon of salt and cook, stirring occasionally, for 10–15 minutes, until the onion is a rich golden brown. Add the ginger and garlic paste and cook, stirring, for 2 minutes or until fragrant. Add the chilli powder, turmeric, cumin, coriander and green chilli and cook for a further 2–3 minutes, until fragrant. Add the passata and 125 ml (½ cup) of water, then bring to the boil over medium heat and simmer, uncovered and stirring frequently, for 1–2 minutes, until the liquid is reduced and slightly thickened.

Stir in the mushroom and cook for 6–8 minutes, until tender, then stir through the peas and fenugreek leaves and bring to a simmer. Cook for 3–4 minutes, until the peas are heated through, adding a little boiling water if the sauce is very thick. Add the garam masala and season to taste with salt.

Serve with steamed basmati rice or naan and yoghurt on the side, if desired.

Paneer Butter Masala

A vegetarian take on butter chicken, paneer butter masala makes a fantastic addition to any Indian banquet, as it's loved by everyone. With delicately soft cottage cheese that melts in your mouth, served in a tangy tomato and cashew gravy doused in cream, what's not to love?

2 tablespoons ghee
2 onions, finely chopped
sea salt
1 tablespoon ginger and garlic
   paste
1 teaspoon chilli powder
1 teaspoon ground turmeric
1 long green chilli, chopped
250 g (1 cup) passata (puréed
   tomatoes)
50 g (⅓ cup) raw cashew nuts
125 ml (½ cup) cream, plus extra
   to serve
20 g (¾ oz) unsalted butter,
   chopped
2 teaspoons honey
1 teaspoon dried fenugreek leaves,
   crushed
400 g (14 oz) paneer cheese, cut
   into 2 cm (¾ in) cubes
small handful of coriander (cilantro),
   roughly chopped, plus extra to
   serve
Simple naan (see page 126), to
   serve

Heat the ghee in a large heavy-based frying pan over medium–low heat. Add the onion and ½ teaspoon of salt and cook, stirring occasionally, for 10–15 minutes, until the onion is a rich golden brown. Add the ginger and garlic paste and cook, stirring, for 2 minutes or until fragrant. Add the chilli powder, turmeric and green chilli and cook for 1 minute. Add the passata and 125 ml (½ cup) of water, then bring to the boil over medium heat and simmer, uncovered and stirring often, for 5–8 minutes, until the tomato is reduced and slightly thickened.

Meanwhile, place the cashews in a small food processor and process until ground.

Add the cream and butter to the tomato mixture and cook, stirring, until the butter is melted. Stir in the ground cashews, honey and fenugreek leaves until well combined and add a little boiling water if the sauce is very thick. Stir in the paneer and coriander and cook, stirring gently, until the paneer is heated through. Season to taste.

Serve drizzled with extra cream and scattered with extra coriander, with naan on the side.

Goan-Style Vegetable Curry

The state of Goa is known for its delicious fish curries, beer and a very chilled-out approach to life. But Goa also has many vegetarian dishes in its culinary repertoire, and this vegetable curry is one of the best. Coconut grows abundantly in the region, and here it adds a subtle, creamy flavour that elevates the dish.

2 tablespoons coconut or
   vegetable oil
300 g (10½ oz) cauliflower, cut
   into florets
1 large potato, peeled and cut into
   1.5 cm (½ in) pieces
1 onion, chopped
1 tomato, finely chopped
1 tablespoon ginger and
   garlic paste
2 small green chillies, sliced
½ teaspoon ground cumin
½ teaspoon ground turmeric
200 ml (7 fl oz) coconut milk
1 large carrot, chopped
150 g (5½ oz) green beans,
   trimmed and sliced
30 g (¼ cup) freshly grated coconut
   (see Note), plus extra to serve
½ teaspoon sea salt
handful of coriander (cilantro),
   chopped, plus extra to serve
1–2 teaspoons tamarind purée,
   to taste
Steamed basmati rice
   (see page 124), to serve

Heat a large frying pan over medium heat and add half the oil. Add the cauliflower and potato and sauté for 4–5 minutes, until lightly browned. Transfer to a plate and set aside.

Add the remaining oil to the pan along with the onion and sauté for 5–6 minutes, until softened. Add the tomato and cook for 2 minutes or until softened, then add the ginger and garlic paste and cook until fragrant. Add the chilli and spices and cook, stirring, for a further 2 minutes or until fragrant.

Add the coconut milk, 250 ml (1 cup) of water, all the vegetables and the grated coconut, and bring to the boil over medium heat. Reduce the heat to a simmer, season with the salt and cook, covered, for 10–12 minutes, until the vegetables are tender. Stir in the chopped coriander and tamarind, to taste.

Scatter with extra coriander and/or extra coconut and serve with steamed basmati rice.

Note: You can also use frozen grated coconut, which can be purchased at Indian grocery stores.

Saag Paneer

Every North Indian grows up eating homemade paneer. The state of Punjab has the highest milk production across India, so it is not surprising that cheese is abundant in Indian homes throughout the region. A popular dish is saag paneer, which is usually made with seasonal winter greens. This recipe uses spinach and the end result is equally delicious.

2 tablespoons ghee
300 g (10½ oz) paneer cheese,
    cut into 1.5 cm (½ in) cubes
sea salt
½ teaspoon black mustard seeds
1 onion, thinly sliced
3 garlic cloves, thinly sliced
2 cm (¾ in) piece of ginger,
    julienned
½ teaspoon chilli powder
½ teaspoon ground turmeric
500 g (1 lb 2 oz) English spinach,
    washed and tough stalks
    removed, leaves roughly
    shredded
¼ teaspoon garam masala
squeeze of lemon juice, to taste
    (optional)

Heat 1 tablespoon of the ghee in a large non-stick frying pan over medium–high heat. Working in batches if necessary, add the paneer and fry for 5–6 minutes, turning so that at least 2–3 sides are well browned. Transfer the paneer to a plate with a slotted spoon and sprinkle lightly with salt.

Heat the remaining ghee in the same frying pan over medium–high heat. Add the mustard seeds and let them sizzle for a few seconds, until they start to crackle. Add the onion, garlic, ginger, chilli and turmeric to the pan and cook, stirring, for 4–5 minutes, until the onion is well coloured.

Add the shredded spinach (in batches if necessary, so that it all fits in the pan), turning constantly with a pair of tongs until wilted. Return the paneer to the pan and stir until hot. Stir in the garam masala, season to taste and add a little lemon juice if you like.

Serve as part of a shared meal with your choice of rice, breads and other curries.

Mathanga Erissery

A delicately spiced curry made with pumpkin and beans, this dish is made during the harvest festival of Onam in the state of Kerala. Cooked in a spicy chilli and coconut paste, it is not only nutritious but also vegan.

600 g (1 lb 5 oz) peeled pumpkin (winter squash), cut into 3 cm (1¼ in) chunks
½ teaspoon ground turmeric
sea salt
60 g (½ cup) freshly grated coconut (or use frozen grated coconut)
2 long green chillies, roughly chopped
2 teaspoons cumin seeds
1 teaspoon Kashmiri chilli powder
400 g (14 oz) tin adzuki beans or red kidney beans, rinsed and drained
Steamed basmati rice (see page 124), to serve

Erissery temper
2 tablespoons coconut oil
½ teaspoon black mustard seeds
2 dried red chillies
2 sprigs curry leaves, leaves stripped
30 g (¼ cup) freshly grated coconut (or use frozen grated coconut)

Place the pumpkin in a saucepan, add the turmeric, a good sprinkle of salt and enough water to barely cover the pumpkin. Stir and bring to the boil over high heat, then reduce the heat to a simmer and cook for 6–8 minutes, until the pumpkin is just tender. Strain the pumpkin, reserving the cooking liquid.

Blend the coconut, the green chilli, cumin seeds and chilli powder in a blender or the small bowl of a food processor to make a paste. Add a little water to get the mixture moving, if necessary.

Return the pumpkin to the pan and add the paste, beans and about 80 ml (⅓ cup) of the reserved cooking liquid. Cook, stirring, over low heat for 8–10 minutes, mashing the pumpkin lightly.

To make the temper, heat the oil in a frying pan over medium heat, add the mustard seeds and when they start to crackle add the dried chillies and curry leaves. Sizzle for a few seconds, then add the coconut. Cook, stirring, for 1–2 minutes, until the coconut is lightly browned. Stir most of the tempered mixture into the pumpkin mixture, then serve with the remainder spooned over the top.

Serve with steamed basmati rice.

Malai Kofta

Malai kofta is an excellent dish to make when entertaining because it never fails to wow everyone. You can either serve the koftas on their own with the sauce on the side for dipping, or stir the koftas through the curry at the end of cooking.

400 g (14 oz) floury potatoes
sea salt
100 g (1 cup) grated paneer cheese
1 tablespoon finely chopped
    cashew nuts
1 tablespoon finely chopped raisins
3 tablespoons cornflour
    (cornstarch)
½ teaspoon garam masala
½ teaspoon chilli powder (optional)
vegetable oil, for deep-frying
60 ml (¼ cup) cream
Steamed basmati rice
    (see page 124), to serve

Malai kofta sauce
80 ml (⅓ cup) vegetable oil
1 onion, finely chopped
1 tablespoon ginger and
    garlic paste
500 g (2 cups) passata (puréed
    tomatoes)
2 tablespoons cashew nuts, finely
    ground
1 teaspoon cumin seeds
1 teaspoon ground coriander
½ teaspoon ground turmeric
1 fresh or dried bay leaf
1 cinnamon stick
4 cloves
3 green cardamom pods, bruised
½ teaspoon dried fenugreek leaves,
    crushed
½ teaspoon garam masala

Peel the potatoes, then transfer to a saucepan, cover with cold water and add a good pinch of salt. Bring to the boil and cook until tender. Drain, then mash and set aside to cool.

Combine the potato, paneer, cashews, raisins, cornflour, garam masala, chilli powder (if using) and ½ teaspoon of salt in a bowl. Knead the mixture into a soft dough, then divide into 12 portions and roll into smooth balls. Set aside.

To make the sauce, heat three-quarters of the oil in a frying pan over low heat. Add the onion and ginger and garlic paste and cook for 10 minutes. Add the passata, ground cashews and 250 ml (1 cup) of water and simmer for 5–7 minutes, until slightly thickened. Season to taste with salt. Transfer the mixture to a food processor and blitz to a smooth sauce. Wipe the pan clean.

Heat the remaining oil in the pan over medium heat and add the cumin seeds, ground coriander, turmeric, bay leaf, cinnamon stick, cloves and cardamom pods and cook, stirring, for 1 minute, until fragrant. Pour the sauce back into the pan and add the fenugreek leaves and garam masala. Gently warm through.

Heat enough oil for deep-frying in a saucepan to 190°C (375°F) on a kitchen thermometer. Working in batches, deep-fry the kofta for 2–3 minutes, until well browned on all sides. Transfer to a plate lined with paper towel to drain, then gently stir through the sauce.

Transfer the malai kofta to a serving dish and drizzle the cream over the top. Serve with steamed basmati rice on the side.

Bhindi Masala

Okra can be a tricky ingredient to cook with due to the mucilaginous nature of the plant. Frying the okra and then cooking it with an acidic ingredient, such as tomato, makes it less gooey, making this bhindi masala a wonderful way to serve this under-appreciated vegetable without having to worry about its texture.

125 ml (½ cup) vegetable or
    peanut oil
500 g (1 lb 2 oz) okra, ends trimmed
1 large onion, finely chopped
1 tablespoon ginger and
    garlic paste
2 teaspoons ground cumin
2 teaspoons ground coriander
1 teaspoon chilli powder
½ teaspoon ground turmeric
4 large tomatoes, roughly chopped
sea salt
1 teaspoon garam masala
small handful of chopped coriander
    (cilantro)
¼–½ teaspoon amchur powder
    (dried green mango powder;
    optional)
Chapattis (see page 131), Simple
    naan (see page 126) or Steamed
    basmati rice (see page 124),
    to serve

Heat 2 tablespoons of the oil in a large deep frying pan over medium–high heat. Add half the okra and cook, stirring occasionally, for 10 minutes, until golden and slightly shrivelled. Remove to a plate. Repeat with another 2 tablespoons of the oil and the remaining okra, then add this okra to the cooked batch.

In the same pan, heat the remaining oil over medium heat. Add the onion and cook for 5–8 minutes, until soft. Add the ginger and garlic paste and spices and cook, stirring, for 2 minutes, until fragrant. Add the tomato, ½ teaspoon of salt, the fried okra and 125 ml (½ cup) of water and cook, covered, for 5 minutes, or until the okra is very soft. Stir in the garam masala, coriander and amchur powder (if using) and season with salt, to taste.

Serve with chapattis, naan or steamed basmati rice.

Aloo Curry

This is one of the easiest curries to make when you don't have the energy to make anything else. Potatoes are popular throughout India as they soak up the flavour of any curry they are cooked in. Try adding frozen peas to this dish for another vegetable element, or serve as part of a larger Indian banquet.

3 tablespoons ghee or vegetable oil
1 teaspoon black mustard seeds
½ teaspoon cumin seeds
1 sprig curry leaves
1 onion, chopped
2 tomatoes, chopped
1 long green chilli, sliced, plus extra
    to serve
2 teaspoons ground coriander
2 teaspoons Kashmiri chilli powder
½ teaspoon ground turmeric
600 g (1 lb 5 oz) waxy potatoes,
    scrubbed and chopped into
    2 cm (¾ in) pieces
1 teaspoon sea salt
125 ml (½ cup) coconut milk
large handful of coriander (cilantro)
    leaves, roughly chopped, plus
    extra to serve
1 teaspoon dried fenugreek leaves,
    crushed
Steamed basmati rice
    (see page 124) or Paratha
    (see page 128), to serve

Heat the ghee or oil in a large non-stick saucepan over medium–high heat. Add the mustard seeds, cumin seeds and curry leaves and sizzle for a few seconds, until they start to crackle. Add the onion, then reduce the heat to medium and cook, stirring, for about 3 minutes, or until the onion has softened. Add the tomato, green chilli and spices and cook, stirring, for 2–3 minutes, until the tomato begins to break down. Add the potato, salt and 250 ml (1 cup) of water. Bring to the boil, then reduce the heat and simmer, covered, for 15–20 minutes, until the potato is tender.

Add the coconut milk, stir well and bring the mixture back to a simmer. Remove from the heat and stir in the coriander and fenugreek leaves.

Serve, topped with the extra chilli and coriander and with steamed basmati rice or paratha on the side.

Sambar

A delightful stew made of vegetables cooked in a lentil-based gravy, sambar is a popular dish from southern India where it is often served with steamed idlis (savoury rice pancakes) or dosas.

250 g (1 cup) masoor dal (split red
    lentils), well rinsed
1 teaspoon Kashmiri chilli powder
sea salt
¼ teaspoon ground turmeric
1 tablespoon vegetable oil
12 small Asian shallots, peeled
100 g (3½ oz) drumstick vegetable,
    scraped clean and sliced
150 g (5½ oz) cauliflower florets
1 small eggplant (aubergine), diced
1 large tomato, diced
2 teaspoons tamarind purée
1–2 teaspoons shaved jaggery
large handful of coriander (cilantro),
    chopped
Steamed basmati rice
    (see page 124), to serve

Sambar masala
4 dried red chillies
1 tablespoon coriander seeds
1 tablespoon chana dal
2.5 cm (1 in) cinnamon stick, broken
1 teaspoon cumin seeds
½ teaspoon fenugreek seeds
1 sprig curry leaves, leaves stripped
1½ tablespoons desiccated coconut
pinch of asafoetida

Sambar temper
1 tablespoon ghee or vegetable oil
½ teaspoon cumin seeds
½ teaspoon mustard seeds
¼ teaspoon fenugreek seeds
1 sprig curry leaves, leaves stripped

To make the sambar masala, combine all of the ingredients except the coconut and asafoetida in a dry frying pan over low heat. Toast, stirring constantly, for 3–4 minutes, until fragrant. Add the coconut and stir for 1–2 minutes, until lightly browned. Allow to cool, then place in a spice grinder and blend to a powder. Stir in the asafoetida. Store in a jar in the pantry for up to 3 months.

Combine the masoor dal, chilli powder, ½ teaspoon of salt, the turmeric and 750 ml (3 cups) of water in a large saucepan over medium heat and bring to the boil. Reduce the heat to a simmer and cook, stirring occasionally, for 25–30 minutes, until the mixture is quite thick.

Heat the oil in a large saucepan over medium heat. Add the vegetables and cook, stirring occasionally, for 3–4 minutes, until lightly coloured. Add the tomato and enough water to barely cover the mixture and stir well. Bring to the boil, then reduce the heat to a simmer and cook for 5 minutes. Add 2 tablespoons of the sambar masala, the tamarind purée and half the jaggery. Simmer until the vegetables are completely tender, then season with salt and stir in the lentils. Cook for 5 minutes, then stir in the coriander and season with more salt, tamarind purée and jaggery if required.

For the sambar temper, heat the ghee or oil in a frying pan over medium heat. Add the seeds and sizzle for a few seconds, then add the curry leaves and sauté for 30 seconds. Pour the temper over the sambar and serve immediately with steamed basmati rice on the side.

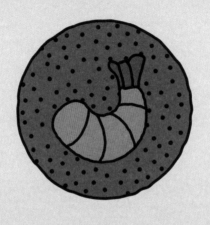

Seafood

Tandoori Fish Tikka Masala

Typically fish tikka is served as an appetiser, but you can also serve it in a tomato masala, which takes the fish to another level. To save time, make the sauce in advance and just scoop it over the hot pieces of fish before serving.

125 g (½ cup) natural yoghurt

3 tablespoons Tandoori curry paste (see page 132)

4 × 150 g (5½ oz) mackerel steaks

2 tablespoons ghee or vegetable oil

1 large onion, thinly sliced

½ teaspoon sea salt

1 tablespoon ginger and garlic paste

1 long red chilli, sliced, plus extra finely chopped to serve

2 teaspoons ground coriander

1 teaspoon Kashmiri chilli powder

1 teaspoon garam masala

½ teaspoon ground turmeric

250 g (1 cup) passata (puréed tomatoes)

125 ml (½ cup) coconut milk, plus extra to serve

25 g (¼ cup) ground almonds

handful of coriander (cilantro) leaves, roughly chopped, plus extra to serve

Steamed basmati rice (see page 124), to serve

Combine the yoghurt and tandoori paste in a large bowl, add the mackerel and toss well to coat. Cover and refrigerate for 1 hour.

Heat a grill (broiler) to high heat and line a baking tray with foil. Place the fish on the prepared tray and grill for 6–8 minutes each side, until charred in spots and barely cooked through.

Meanwhile, heat the ghee or oil in a large heavy-based frying pan over medium–low heat. Add the onion and salt and cook, stirring occasionally, for 10–15 minutes, until the onion is a rich golden brown. Add the ginger and garlic paste and red chilli and cook, stirring, for 2 minutes or until fragrant. Add the spices and cook for 1 minute, then add the passata, coconut milk, ground almonds and 125 ml (½ cup) of water and bring to the boil. Reduce the heat to a simmer and cook, uncovered and stirring frequently, for 6–8 minutes, until the sauce is reduced and slightly thickened. Stir in the coriander.

Add the fish and spoon the sauce over the top. Cook gently for a few minutes, until the fish is cooked through. Season to taste.

Drizzle with extra coconut milk and scatter over the extra coriander and red chilli. Serve with steamed basmati rice on the side.

Kerala-Style Fish Curry

There are many ways in which fish is cooked in Kerala, but they nearly all include coconut in some form or another due to the abundance of this sweet fruit. This recipe has a subtle taste and is not overtly spicy. The fish soaks up the goodness of the lightly spiced coconut gravy and goes really well with basmati rice.

600 g (1 lb 5 oz) thick firm white fish fillets, cut into 3 cm (1¼ in) pieces
sea salt
1 teaspoon ground turmeric
2 tablespoons melted coconut oil
1 sprig curry leaves, leaves stripped
2 Asian shallots, sliced
3 cm (1¼ in) piece of ginger, julienned
1 long red chilli, thinly sliced
½ teaspoon chilli powder
1 tablespoon sweet paprika
1–2 teaspoons tamarind purée, to taste
freshly ground black pepper
300 ml (10½ fl oz) coconut milk
chopped coriander (cilantro) leaves, to serve
Steamed basmati rice (see page 124), to serve

Sprinkle the fish with a little salt and ¼ teaspoon of the turmeric and toss gently to coat. Cover and set aside.

Heat the coconut oil in a large frying pan over medium–high heat. Add the curry leaves and sizzle for a few seconds, then add the shallot and cook, stirring occasionally, for 4–5 minutes, or until starting to brown. Add the ginger and sliced chilli and cook for 1 minute until fragrant. Add 250 ml (1 cup) of water, the remaining turmeric, chilli powder, paprika and 1 teaspoon of the tamarind purée. Season generously with salt and pepper, then reduce the heat to low and simmer, stirring occasionally, for 5 minutes. Add the coconut milk and bring back to a simmer.

Add the fish to the sauce, stir gently and cook, spooning the sauce over the fish so that it cooks evenly, for 8–10 minutes, until just cooked through. Taste, and season with a little more tamarind purée to balance the flavour if necessary.

Scatter with coriander and serve with steamed basmati rice.

Goan-Style Prawn Curry

Goans are very proud of their prawn curries and when you make this you'll see why. The key to this dish is to ensure that the prawns are not overcooked. Served with lime wedges for extra zing, you'll be going back for seconds and licking your fingers after polishing this off!

1 tablespoon peanut oil
1 onion, finely chopped
1 small tomato, finely chopped
1 tablespoon ginger and
    garlic paste
2 teaspoons sweet paprika
1 teaspoon ground coriander
½ teaspoon ground cumin
½ teaspoon freshly ground
    black pepper
½ teaspoon cayenne pepper
300 ml (10½ fl oz) coconut milk
1 kg (2 lb 3 oz) raw prawns
    (shrimp), peeled and deveined
    with tails left intact
½ teaspoon sea salt
1–2 teaspoons tamarind purée,
    to taste

To serve
coriander (cilantro) leaves
Steamed basmati rice
    (see page 124)
lime wedges

Heat the oil in a large frying pan over medium heat. Add the onion and cook, stirring occasionally, for 6–8 minutes, until softened and starting to brown. Add the tomato and cook for 2 minutes, or until softened. Add the ginger and garlic paste and cook until fragrant. Add the spices and cook, stirring, for a further 2 minutes.

Add the coconut milk and bring to the boil, then reduce the heat to a simmer and add the prawns, salt and tamarind purée. Stir and cook for 4–5 minutes, until the prawns are just cooked through.

Scatter with coriander leaves and serve with steamed basmati rice and lime wedges for squeezing over.

Dahi Machi

Yoghurt is a popular ingredient in Indian cuisine, but it can be tricky to cook with as there is always the risk of it splitting when it comes into contact with heat. To avoid this, try mixing the yoghurt with a little water before adding it to the curry. Not only will it stop the mixture from separating, it will help give the final dish a silky texture and robust flavour.

600 g (1 lb 5 oz) thick firm
    white fish fillets, cut into
    4 cm (1½ in) pieces
sea salt
1½ teaspoons ground turmeric
2 tablespoons mustard oil or
    vegetable oil
1 small onion, puréed
2 teaspoons finely grated ginger
1 teaspoon chilli powder
¼ teaspoon ground cinnamon
250 g (1 cup) natural yoghurt
handful of coriander (cilantro)
    leaves
1–2 small green chillies, finely
    chopped
Steamed basmati rice
    (see page 124), to serve

Sprinkle the fish with a little salt and ½ teaspoon of the turmeric and toss gently to coat. Set aside for 15 minutes.

Heat the mustard oil or vegetable oil in a large frying pan over medium–high heat until smoking. Reduce the heat slightly, then, working in batches, add the fish and cook for 2–3 minutes, until browned all over, but not cooked through. Transfer to a plate with a slotted spoon and set aside.

Add the onion purée and ½ teaspoon of salt to the pan and cook, stirring occasionally, for 10–12 minutes, until starting to brown. Add the ginger, remaining turmeric, chilli powder, cinnamon and 1 tablespoon of water. Cook for 2–3 minutes, until fragrant, then reduce the heat to medium–low and add 125 ml (½ cup) of water and the yoghurt. Slowly bring to a simmer, stirring contstantly.

Add the fish to the sauce, stir gently and simmer for 3–4 minutes, until the fish is just cooked through. Season to taste.

Scatter with the coriander leaves and green chilli, and serve with steamed basmati rice.

SERVES 4

Mussels in Curry Sauce

In Goa, mussels are called xinaneao and they are extremely popular. Walk up to any of the shacks dotted on the pristine beaches and you will find vendors selling mussels cooked in their own specialty curry sauce. This rendition is light and tangy, allowing the delicate flavour of the mussels to shine.

3 tablespoons ghee or vegetable oil
3 onions, finely chopped
sea salt
1 tablespoon ginger and
    garlic paste
2 long green chillies, deseeded
    and chopped, plus extra sliced
    chilli to serve
1 teaspoon ground turmeric
1 tablespoon ground coriander
1 tomato, chopped
large handful of coriander (cilantro),
    stalks and leaves chopped
    separately
1 kg (2 lb 3 oz) mussels, scrubbed
    and debearded
Steamed basmati rice (see page
    124) or Paratha (see page 128),
    to serve

Heat the ghee or oil in a large heavy-based saucepan over medium–low heat. Add the onion and ½ teaspoon of salt and cook, stirring frequently, for 15–20 minutes, until golden. Add the ginger and garlic paste, chilli, turmeric and ground coriander and cook, stirring, for 2–3 minutes, until fragrant. Stir in the tomato, coriander stalks and 250 ml (1 cup) of water, then bring to the boil, cover and simmer for 5 minutes. Season to taste.

Stir in the mussels, then cover and cook, shaking the pan and giving the mixture a stir every 30 seconds. Quickly scoop out any mussels that are open and place in a large bowl. As soon as all the mussels are open (discard any that don't), return all the open mussels to the pan and bring the mixture to a gentle simmer. Scatter with the coriander leaves and sliced chilli.

Serve immediately with steamed basmati rice or paratha.

Prawn Malai

Bengal's seafood dishes are legendary and this prawn malai curry is no exception: thick, juicy prawns cooked in a delicate coconut gravy until silky smooth. What's not to love? Even better, this dish can be made in less than 20 minutes. It doesn't get easier (or more delicious) than this.

60 ml (¼ cup) mustard oil or ghee
1 large cinnamon stick
2 fresh or dried bay leaves
2 onions, finely chopped
2 tablespoons ginger and
    garlic paste
1 teaspoon cumin seeds
1 teaspoon Kashmiri chilli powder
2 teaspoons ground turmeric
24 large raw prawns (shrimp),
    peeled and deveined, tails
    left intact
500 ml (2 cups) coconut milk
1 teaspoon sea salt
½ teaspoon sugar
1 teaspoon garam masala
lime or lemon wedges, to serve
Steamed basmati rice
    (see page 124), to serve

Heat the oil in a heavy-based saucepan or large frying pan over medium heat. Add the cinnamon stick and bay leaves and cook for 1 minute. Reduce the heat to low, add the onion and cook for 10 minutes, until soft and slightly coloured. Add the ginger and garlic paste and cook for a further 2 minutes. Add the cumin seeds, chilli powder and turmeric along with the prawns and stir for 1 minute. Add the coconut milk, 80 ml (⅓ cup) of water, the salt and sugar and simmer for 5 minutes or until the prawns are cooked through. Sprinkle over the garam masala.

Serve with lime or lemon wedges for squeezing over and steamed basmati rice on the side.

Bengali Fish Curry

Bengalis love their fish. Whether it's served for lunch or dinner, at an engagement or wedding, fish will always appear on the menu. This recipe is one of the simplest to make. The mustard paste gives the dish a slight wasabi-like kick, without overpowering the delicate fish. The best way to eat it is to ditch that cutlery and use your fingers.

4 × 150 g–200 g (5½ oz–7 oz) mackerel steaks
sea salt
1 teaspoon ground turmeric
¾ teaspoon black mustard seeds
½ teaspoon yellow mustard seeds
1 small onion, roughly chopped
6 small green chillies or 4 long green chillies
60 ml (¼ cup) mustard oil or vegetable oil
4 fresh or dried bay leaves
lemon wedges, to serve
Steamed basmati rice (see page 124), to serve

Rub the fish with a sprinkling of salt and half the turmeric.

Grind the mustard seeds in a spice grinder or with a mortar and pestle. Blend the ground mustard seeds, onion and half the chillies in the small bowl of a food processor or blender to a smooth paste. Add a small amount of water to get the mixture moving, if necessary.

Heat the oil in a frying pan over medium–high heat. Cook the fish for 1–2 minutes each side or until lightly browned. Transfer to a plate.

Add the onion paste, remaining turmeric, ½ teaspoon of salt and the bay leaves to the pan, then reduce the heat to medium and cook for 3 minutes or until fragrant. Add 375 ml (1½ cups) of water and bring to the boil. Simmer for 5 minutes, then return the fish to the pan and add the remaining chillies. Reduce the heat to medium–low and simmer, covered, for 5–6 minutes, until the fish is just cooked through. Season with a little more salt, if necessary.

Serve with lemon wedges and steamed basmati rice.

Chicken

Classic Butter Chicken

One of the most recognised Indian dishes throughout the world, a well made butter chicken will make your taste buds sing. The secret to this dish lies in the sauce, and if you learn to make this right, you will always be super impressed with the results.

8 (about 1.5 kg/3 lb 5 oz) skin-on chicken thigh cutlets
125 g (½ cup) natural yoghurt
3 tablespoons Tandoori curry paste (see page 132)
2 tablespoons ghee
2 tablespoons vegetable oil
2 large onions, chopped
1 teaspoon sea salt
1 tablespoon ginger and garlic paste
1 teaspoon chilli powder
2 teaspoons ground turmeric
1 long green chilli, chopped
425 g (15 oz) passata (puréed tomatoes)
180 ml (6½ fl oz) cream
40 g (1½ oz) unsalted butter, chopped
75 g (½ cup) raw cashew nuts
4 teaspoons honey
1 tablespoon dried fenugreek leaves, crushed
small handful of coriander (cilantro), roughly chopped
Simple naan (see page 126), to serve

Using a sharp knife, cut the chicken cutlets in half. Combine the chicken, yoghurt and tandoori curry paste in a large bowl. Cover and refrigerate for 30 minutes or, preferably, overnight.

Heat a chargrill pan or heavy-based frying pan over high heat. Shake the excess marinade from the chicken and cook for 3–4 minutes each side, until well charred in spots, but not cooked through. Transfer to a plate and set aside.

Meanwhile, heat the ghee and oil in a large heavy-based frying pan over medium–low heat. Add the onion and salt and cook, stirring occasionally, for 10–15 minutes, until the onion is a rich golden brown. Add the ginger and garlic paste and cook, stirring, for 2 minutes or until fragrant. Add the chilli powder, turmeric and green chilli and cook for a further 1 minute. Add the passata, then bring to the boil over medium heat and simmer, uncovered and stirring often, for 5–10 minutes, until the passata is reduced and slightly thickened. Add the cream and butter and cook, stirring, until the butter is melted.

Place the cashew nuts in the small bowl of a food processor and process until finely ground, then add to the pan. Add the charred chicken, honey and fenugreek leaves and cook, stirring frequently, for 5–6 minutes, until the chicken is cooked through. Stir in the coriander and season, to taste.

Serve with naan on the side.

Tandoori Chicken

A tandoor is a clay oven set into the earth and fired with wood or charcoal. It can reach eye-watering temperatures of up to 480°C (900°F), allowing marinated meat to cook very quickly. Unfortunately, not many of us will have a tandoor in the back garden, but you can still rustle up this delicious tandoori chicken using a domestic oven.

1.5 kg (3 lb 5 oz) whole chicken
180 g (¾ cup) natural yoghurt
125 g (½ cup) Tandoori curry paste
   (see page 132)
coriander (cilantro) leaves, to serve
lemon wedges, to serve
Simple naan (see page 126), to
   serve

First, butterfly or flatten the chicken. Using kitchen scissors, cut along both sides of the backbone and remove. Turn the chicken over and place on a clean work surface. Using the heel of your hand, press down firmly on the breastbone to flatten.

Slash the chicken about 1 cm (½ in) deep through the thickest parts of the breast, thighs and legs.

Combine the yoghurt and tandoori curry paste in a bowl, then rub all over the chicken, rubbing well into the slashed areas. Transfer to a baking tray lined with baking paper, then cover and marinate in the fridge for 2–4 hours.

Preheat the oven to 240°C (465°F) fan-forced.

Roast the chicken for 30 minutes or until it starts to char in spots. Reduce the oven temperature to 150°C (300°F) and continue to roast the chicken for 5–10 minutes, until cooked through. Remove from the oven and set aside to rest, covered loosely with foil, for 10 minutes.

Scatter the coriander over the chicken and serve with lemon wedges for squeezing over and naan on the side.

Chicken Balti

The origin of this dish is unknown and there are many stories about where it comes from. However, balti refers to the cookware in which the chicken is cooked, and there is a culture of cooking in cast-iron pans and woks in South Asian communities, due to the health benefits of the metal. This makes the resulting dish rich, not just in colour but also flavour.

2 tablespoons ghee or vegetable oil
2 teaspoons black mustard seeds
1 red capsicum (bell pepper), cut
    into 1.5 cm (½ in) pieces
1 large onion, chopped
4 long green chillies, halved
    lengthways
1 fresh or dried bay leaf
2 tablespoons ginger and
    garlic paste
400 g (14 oz) tin crushed tomatoes
60 g (¼ cup) natural yoghurt
1 tablespoon besan (chickpea flour)
2 teaspoons garam masala
2 teaspoons ground coriander
2 teaspoons ground cumin
1 teaspoon Kashmiri chilli powder
1 teaspoon ground turmeric
sea salt
600 g (1 lb 5 oz) skinless chicken
    thigh fillets, cut into 2.5 cm (1 in)
    pieces
squeeze of lemon juice, to taste
freshly ground black pepper
coriander (cilantro) leaves, roughly
    chopped, to serve
Steamed basmati rice
    (see page 124), to serve

Heat the ghee or oil in a large heavy-based saucepan over medium heat. Add the mustard seeds and sizzle for a few seconds. When they start to crackle, add the capsicum, onion, green chilli and bay leaf. Cook, stirring occasionally, for 10–12 minutes, until the vegetables are golden and starting to stick to the base of the pan. Add the ginger and garlic paste and cook, stirring, for about 30 seconds, until fragrant. Add the tomatoes, yoghurt, besan, spices and ½ teaspoon of salt and stir until well combined. Bring to the boil, then reduce the heat to medium–low and simmer for 10 minutes or until slightly thickened. Add the chicken and stir well to coat in the sauce. Return the mixture to the boil over medium heat, then reduce the heat to a simmer and cook, covered and stirring occasionally, for 15–20 minutes, until the chicken is cooked through and the sauce has thickened.

Season to taste with lemon juice, black pepper and a little more salt, if necessary.

Scatter the curry with the coriander leaves and serve with steamed basmati rice on the side.

Chicken Tikka Masala

Who doesn't love chicken tikka masala? Every single Indian restaurant in the UK has this dish on their menu and they all claim to make the best version of it. The key to a good tikka masala is to ensure that the chicken is grilled until tender and juicy, so that when you add it to the tomato sauce it soaks up all the flavour.

1 kg (2 lb 3 oz) skinless chicken thigh fillets, cut into 4 cm (1½ in) pieces

125 g (½ cup) natural yoghurt, plus extra to serve

3 tablespoons Tandoori curry paste (see page 132)

2 tablespoons ghee

2 tablespoons vegetable oil

2 onions, chopped

1½ tablespoons ginger and garlic paste

2 long green chillies, sliced

sea salt

1 tablespoon ground coriander

2 teaspoons ground turmeric

2 teaspoons sweet paprika

1 teaspoon garam masala

400 g (14 oz) tin crushed tomatoes

400 ml (13½ fl oz) coconut milk

60 g (½ cup) ground almonds

small handful of coriander (cilantro), roughly chopped

2 tablespoons flaked almonds, toasted

Steamed basmati rice (see page 124) and papadams, to serve

Combine the chicken, yoghurt and tandoori curry paste in a large bowl. Cover and refrigerate for 30 minutes to 2 hours.

Heat a chargrill pan or heavy-based frying pan over high heat. Shake the excess marinade from the chicken and cook for 3–4 minutes each side, until well charred in spots, but not cooked through. Transfer to a plate and set aside.

Heat the ghee and oil in a large heavy-based frying pan over medium–low heat. Add the onion, ginger and garlic paste, green chilli and ½ teaspoon of salt and cook, stirring occasionally, for 10–15 minutes, until the onion is a rich golden brown. Add the spices and cook, stirring, for 1 minute or until fragrant. Add the tomatoes, then bring to the boil over medium heat and simmer, uncovered and stirring frequently, for 5–10 minutes, until slightly thickened. Stir in the coconut milk and simmer for a further 15–20 minutes, until the mixture has thickened.

Stir in the ground almonds and charred chicken and cook, stirring frequently, for 5–6 minutes, until the chicken is cooked through. Stir in the coriander and season to taste.

Scatter the flaked almonds over the top and serve with steamed basmati rice and papadams on the side.

SERVES 4–6

Chicken Jalfrezi

Jalfrezi comes from humble beginnings. It was invented as a way to use up leftover roast meat, which was cooked with Indian spices to make it more flavourful. Today, there are many varieties of jalfrezi and most people no longer use leftover meat. This is a very simple recipe that doesn't require many spices, but still packs a punch.

1 kg (2 lb 3 oz) skinless chicken thigh fillets, cut into 3 cm (1¼ in) chunks
1½ tablespoons ground cumin
1½ tablespoons ground coriander
1 tablespoon ground turmeric
80 ml (⅓ cup) vegetable oil
1 large onion, finely chopped
2 tablespoons ginger and garlic paste
1 red capsicum (bell pepper), sliced
1 green capsicum (bell pepper), sliced
3 long green chillies, finely chopped
2 × 400 g (14 oz) tins chopped tomatoes
½–1 teaspoon sea salt, to taste
2 teaspoons garam masala
coriander (cilantro) leaves, chopped, to serve
Steamed basmati rice (see page 124) or papadams, to serve

Combine the chicken with the spices in a large bowl. Set aside for 10 minutes.

Heat the oil in a large heavy-based saucepan or flameproof casserole dish (Dutch oven) over high heat. Working in two batches, add the chicken and brown on all sides. Using a slotted spoon, transfer the chicken to a plate. Add the onion, ginger and garlic paste, capsicums and chilli to the pan and cook, stirring frequently, for 5 minutes, until the vegetables have softened.

Add the tomatoes and 250 ml (1 cup) of water and simmer over low heat for 5 minutes. Add the chicken and simmer for a further 15–20 minutes, until the chicken is tender. Season with the salt and sprinkle in the garam masala.

Scatter the coriander over the top of the curry and serve with steamed basmati rice or papadams on the side.

Hyderabadi Chicken

Hyderabad is known for its biryani, and people flock to their favourite places to eat it. But there are many other dishes in this cuisine that are equally delicious, and this chicken curry is no exception. The addition of cashews gives Hyderabadi chicken a certain amount of richness without being too heavy.

8 × 150 g (5½ oz) chicken
    drumsticks
200 g (7 oz) natural yoghurt
1 teaspoon chilli powder
sea salt
2 large onions, chopped
2 tablespoons ginger and
    garlic paste
50 g (⅓ cup) raw cashew nuts
80 ml (⅓ cup) vegetable oil
1 tablespoon garam masala
400 g (14 oz) tin chopped tomatoes
1 teaspoon ground turmeric
lemon wedges, to serve
Simple naan (see page 126)
    and Steamed basmati rice
    (see page 124), to serve

Combine the chicken, yoghurt, chilli powder and a pinch of salt in a large bowl. Set aside to marinate for at least 30 minutes.

Place the onion and ginger and garlic paste in a food processor and blend to a paste. Transfer to a bowl. Blend the cashews with a splash of water to form a paste.

Heat the oil in a large frying pan or heavy-based saucepan over medium heat. Add the onion paste and cook, stirring occasionally, for 5 minutes or until soft. Add the garam masala and cook, stirring, for 2 minutes. Add the tomatoes and turmeric and cook for 4–5 minutes, until the oil starts to separate. Add the chicken and its marinade to the pan, along with the nut paste and 125 ml (½ cup) of water. Stir to combine, then gently simmer for 15–20 minutes, until the chicken is tender. Season with salt, to taste.

Serve with lemon wedges for squeezing over, and naan and steamed basmati rice on the side.

Chicken Chettinad

A very popular chicken preparation from the region of Chettinad in Tamil Nadu, which is known for using whole spices in rich, flavoursome curries that can blow your socks off. Feel free to tone down the spice levels depending on your personal preference, or use the recommended amount of spice and enjoy it as the locals do.

1 kg (2 lb 3 oz) skinless chicken
   thigh cutlets
125 ml (½ cup) buttermilk
1 tablespoon ground turmeric
80 ml (⅓ cup) coconut or
   vegetable oil
2.5 cm (1 in) cinnamon stick
3 green cardamom pods, cracked
2 cloves
250 g (9 oz) shallots, thinly sliced
25 g (¼ cup) desiccated coconut
90 g (3 oz) ginger and garlic paste
1 tablespoon Kashmiri chilli powder
1½ tablespoons ground coriander
400 g (14 oz) tin chopped tomatoes
2 large handfuls of coriander
   (cilantro), chopped
2 sprigs curry leaves, leaves
   stripped
1 teaspoon freshly ground
   black pepper
sea salt
Steamed basmati rice
   (see page 124) or Paratha
   (see page 128), to serve

Combine the chicken, buttermilk and 1 teaspoon of the turmeric in a bowl and set aside.

Heat the oil in a large heavy-based saucepan over medium heat. Add the cinnamon, cardamom and cloves and cook for 30 seconds or until fragrant. Add the shallot, then reduce the heat a little and cook, stirring frequently, for 10–12 minutes, until golden brown. Add the coconut and ginger and garlic paste and cook for about 10 minutes, until the mixture is dark golden. Add the chilli powder, ground coriander and remaining turmeric and cook for about 1 minute, until fragrant, then add the tomatoes and 125 ml (½ cup) of water. Cover and simmer for 10–15 minutes, until slightly thickened.

Stir in the chicken mixture and cook, partially covered and stirring occasionally, for 15–20 minutes, until the chicken is cooked through. Stir through the coriander, curry leaves and pepper and season with salt to taste.

Serve with steamed basmati rice or paratha.

Chicken Dopiaza

A mouthwatering preparation in which onions are added in two different ways to the chicken sauce. The key is to slowly cook the onion until it is caramelised to add depth to the overall dish. This is a simple, yet flavourful, curry that makes excellent leftovers for lunch or dinner the next day.

6 onions
3 tablespoons ghee
3 tablespoons vegetable oil
2 teaspoons sea salt
4 long green chillies, deseeded
1½ tablespoons ginger and
    garlic paste
1 tablespoon ground cumin
1 tablespoon ground coriander
2 teaspoons ground turmeric
1 teaspoon ground cinnamon
½ teaspoon ground cardamom
3 tablespoons tomato paste
    (concentrated purée)
1.2 kg (2 lb 10 oz) chicken
    drumsticks, skin removed
400 g (14 oz) tin chopped tomatoes
60 g (¼ cup) natural yoghurt
Steamed basmati rice
    (see page 124) or Paratha
    (see page 128), to serve

Thinly slice half the onions, then heat the ghee and oil in a large heavy-based saucepan over medium–low heat. Add the sliced onion and ½ teaspoon of the salt and gently cook for 15–20 minutes, until golden. Transfer to a plate with a slotted spoon, leaving the oil mixture in the pan.

Meanwhile, chop the remaining onions and blend or process with the chillies, ginger and garlic paste and spices to a purée. Transfer to the pan and cook for 10–15 minutes, until the colour deepens and the mixture is fragrant. Stir in the tomato paste and cook for a further 2 minutes, then add the chicken, tomatoes, yoghurt, remaining salt and 125 ml (½ cup) of water. Stir well and bring to a simmer over medium heat, then reduce the heat to low, cover and cook for 20–25 minutes, until the chicken is cooked through.

Stir in most of the sliced onion and cook for a further 5–6 minutes, until the sauce thickens slightly.

Scatter the remaining onion over the curry and serve with steamed basmati rice or paratha.

Dhaba-Style Chicken

If you ever visit India and travel through the northern states, you will find the highways dotted with small roadside eateries, known as dhabas, which serve simple and delicious food to weary travellers. This chicken curry was invented at one of these eateries, and it has since become hugely popular.

1 kg (2 lb 3 oz) skinless chicken
   thigh cutlets and drumsticks
125 g (½ cup) natural yoghurt
1 tablespoon ginger and
   garlic paste
1 teaspoon sea salt
3 tablespoons ghee or vegetable oil
1 teaspoon cumin seeds
2 fresh or dried bay leaves
2 red onions, chopped
2 teaspoons Kashmiri chilli powder
2 teaspoons ground coriander
1 teaspoon ground turmeric
½ teaspoon freshly ground
   black pepper
2 tomatoes, roughly chopped
2 teaspoons dried fenugreek
   leaves, crushed
½ teaspoon garam masala
large handful of chopped
   coriander (cilantro)
Steamed basmati rice (see
   page 124), to serve

Dhaba-style temper
1 tablespoon ghee
2 small green chillies, split
   lengthways
2 cm (¾ in) piece of ginger, cut
   into thin matchsticks

Combine the chicken, yoghurt, ginger and garlic paste and salt in a bowl and set aside in the fridge for 1 hour.

Heat the ghee or oil in a large heavy-based saucepan over medium heat. Add the cumin seeds and bay leaves and sizzle for 30 seconds. Add the onion, reduce the heat to medium–low and cook, stirring occasionally, for 8–10 minutes, until softened. Add all the spices, except for the fenugreek and garam masala, and cook for 1 minute or until fragrant, then add the chicken mixture and cook, stirring occasionally, for about 5 minutes or until the chicken changes colour. Stir in the tomato and 80 ml (⅓ cup) of water, then bring to the boil, reduce the heat to low and simmer, covered, for 10 minutes. Give the mixture a stir, then continue to cook, partially covered and stirring occasionally, for a further 10–15 minutes, until the chicken is cooked through. Stir in the fenugreek, garam masala and coriander and simmer for a minute or two more. Season to taste.

For the temper, heat the ghee in a small saucepan over medium heat. Add the chilli and ginger and sizzle for a few seconds until fragrant, then spoon over the curry.

Serve with steamed basmati rice.

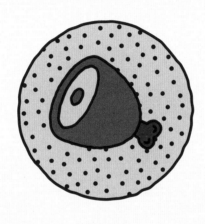

Pork & Beef

Pork Vindaloo

Another popular dish from Goa, vindaloo came to India via the Portuguese and the name basically means meat with vinegar and garlic. The vinegar would flavour and preserve the meat, enabling it to survive long sea voyages between the two countries. However, Goan cooks ultimately made the dish their own by adding locally produced palm vinegar and spices.

1 kg (2 lb 3 oz) pork scotch fillet (neck) or other stewing pork, cut into 3 cm (1¼ in) pieces

1 x quantity Vindaloo curry paste (see page 132)

125 ml (½ cup) coconut vinegar or 2 tablespoons white vinegar

3 tablespoons ghee or vegetable oil

1 teaspoon black mustard seeds

1 sprig curry leaves, leaves stripped

2 onions, finely chopped

2 tomatoes, finely chopped

1 fresh or dried bay leaf

1 teaspoon sea salt

Steamed basmati rice (see page 124), to serve

Combine the pork, curry paste and vinegar in a large bowl. Cover, refrigerate and marinate for at least 2 hours or overnight.

Heat the ghee or oil in a large heavy-based saucepan over medium heat. Add the mustard seeds and curry leaves and sizzle for a few seconds. When the seeds start to crackle, add the onion, then reduce the heat to medium–low and cook, stirring occasionally, for 10–12 minutes, until the onion is golden brown. Add the tomato, bay leaf and the pork with its marinade to the pan. Stir well and add just enough water to cover.

Bring to the boil, then reduce the heat to low, cover and cook, stirring occasionally, for 1–1½ hours, until the meat is tender and the sauce has thickened slightly. If necessary, remove the lid and continue to cook, uncovered, for a further 15–20 minutes, to reduce the sauce to the desired consistency. Season with the salt.

Serve with steamed basmati rice.

Goan Pork Sausage Curry

Just like the famed vindaloo, Goans also learned how to preserve meat through making sausages. The goan choriz, a spicy sausage made with minced (ground) pork, hot chillies, vinegar and a plethora of spices, is extremely popular. If you can't find the real deal at your local Indian supermarket, substitute Portuguese sausages instead.

300 g (10½ oz) Goan pork sausages (or Portuguese chouriço)
2 tablespoons peanut oil, plus extra if necessary
2 potatoes (about 400 g/14 oz), cut into 1.5 cm (½ in) pieces
1 onion, sliced
2 teaspoons ginger and garlic paste
1 tablespoon tomato paste (concentrated purée)
400 g (14 oz) tin chopped tomatoes
1 small green capsicum (bell pepper), cut into 1.5 cm (½ in) pieces
1 long green chilli, sliced
lime pickle, to serve
4 soft white bread rolls, to serve

Remove the sausage meat from the casings and coarsely crumble into 1.5–2 cm (½–¾ in) pieces. Place the meat in a large dry frying pan and set over medium heat. Cook, stirring occasionally, for 5–10 minutes, until the oil starts to release from the sausage meat and the meat browns. Using a slotted spoon, transfer the meat to a plate. Heat 1 tablespoon of the peanut oil in the same pan and add the potato. Cook, stirring occasionally, for 3–4 minutes, until it starts to gain a bit of colour. Transfer the potato to the plate with the sausage meat.

Add the remaining oil to the pan, along with the onion and ginger and garlic paste and cook, stirring, for 2–3 minutes, until fragrant. Add the tomato paste and cook, stirring constantly, for 30 seconds, then add the tomatoes and 375 ml (1½ cups) of water.

Bring to the boil, return the sausage meat and potato to the pan and add the capsicum and chilli. Reduce the heat to a simmer and cook, covered, for 15–20 minutes, until the potato is tender and the mixture has thickened (add a little more water during cooking if the mixture starts to stick to the base of the pan).

Serve with lime pickle and soft white bread rolls on the side.

Pork Sorpotel

Another gem of Goan cuisine, pork sorpotel is usually eaten a few days after it is cooked to allow the flavours to intensify. The spicy, tangy gravy and fatty pork make this dish the perfect hangover food!

1 kg (2 lb 3 oz) fatty boneless pork, such as skinless belly (a bit of skin is okay) or shoulder, cut into large chunks
sea salt
1 teaspoon ground turmeric
vegetable oil (if needed)
2 red onions, finely chopped
1 small green chilli, split in half lengthways
2 teaspoons grated jaggery or brown sugar
2 teaspoons tamarind purée
sugar, to taste
Simple naan (see page 126), to serve

Sorpotel masala
2 tablespoons Kashmiri chilli powder
8 garlic cloves
3 cm (1¼ in) piece of ginger, roughly chopped
½ teaspoon ground turmeric
½ teaspoon cumin seeds
½ teaspoon ground cinnamon
pinch of freshly ground black pepper
pinch of ground cloves
1–2 tablespoons white or brown vinegar, plus extra to taste

Place the pork, 1 teaspoon of salt and the turmeric in a large saucepan over medium–high heat and add enough water to cover the meat. Bring to the boil, then reduce the heat to a simmer, cover and cook for 35–40 minutes, until the pork is just tender.

Meanwhile, process the masala ingredients in a food processor, using enough vinegar to make a smooth paste.

Strain the pork, reserving the cooking liquid. When cool enough to handle, chop the pork into roughly 1 cm (½ in) pieces.

Heat a large heavy-based saucepan over medium heat. Working in batches, add the pork to the pan and increase the heat slowly until the fat starts to render from the meat. Cook for 3–4 minutes, until well browned. Remove each batch with a slotted spoon, leaving the rendered fat behind. Add a little vegetable oil if the mixture is sticking to the pan.

Add the onion to the pan, reduce the heat to medium–low and cook for 8–10 minutes, until starting to caramelise. Stir in the sorpotel masala, chilli, jaggery and tamarind and cook, stirring, for 2–3 minutes. Return the pork to the pan, along with 500 ml (2 cups) of the reserved cooking liquid. Bring to the boil, then reduce the heat to a simmer and cook for 10–15 minutes, until the sauce thickens. Season to taste with salt, sugar and vinegar.

Serve with naan bread.

Beef Madras

A hangover from the British occupation of India, the red-tinged curries that you often find in many Indian takeaway restaurants come from the Madras curry paste, which is named after the city of the same name. Don't let the fieriness of the dish put you off, as you can simply adjust the spice levels to your own liking.

2 tablespoons ground coriander
1 tablespoon ground cumin
2 teaspoons chilli powder
1 teaspoon ground turmeric
1 teaspoon freshly ground
    black pepper
1 teaspoon black mustard seeds
½ teaspoon sea salt
1 tablespoon ginger and
    garlic paste
2–3 tablespoons white vinegar
3 tablespoons ghee
2 onions, sliced
1 kg (2 lb 3 oz) chuck steak or other
    stewing beef, cut into 2.5 cm
    (1 in) pieces
400 g (14 oz) tin crushed tomatoes
Steamed basmati rice
    (see page 124), to serve
natural yoghurt, to serve

Combine the ground spices, mustard seeds, salt and ginger and garlic paste in a bowl with enough vinegar to form a paste.

Heat 2 tablespoons of the ghee in a heavy-based saucepan over medium heat. Add the spice paste and cook, stirring constantly, for 2–3 minutes, until fragrant. Using a spoon, carefully transfer the spice paste to a large heatproof bowl, leaving any ghee behind.

Add the remaining ghee to the pan, along with the onion. Cook, stirring, for 3–4 minutes, until the onion is soft and golden. Scoop out the onion and add it to the cooked spice paste.

Increase the heat to high. Working in batches, add the beef to the pan and sear for 2–3 minutes, until browned. Transfer to the bowl.

Return all the beef, onion and spice paste to the pan. Cook, stirring, for 1 minute or until the meat is well-coated in the paste. Add the tomatoes and 125 ml (½ cup) of water, then reduce the heat to medium and bring to the boil. Reduce the heat to low, cover and cook, stirring occasionally, for 1¾ hours or until the beef is tender. Add a little extra water if the meat starts to stick to the base of the pan.

Remove the lid and cook, uncovered, for a further 15 minutes or until the sauce has reduced and thickened slightly.

Serve with steamed basmati rice and natural yoghurt.

Bengali Beef Curry

Unlike most Indian curries, this beef curry doesn't use any tomatoes. The style of cooking used to make the dish is called kosha (to sauté) in Bengali. Meat is cooked over a low flame with onions and whole spices until it gains a dark-brown texture and falls off the bone. In India, this curry is normally made with goat and you can substitute it here if you prefer.

80 ml (⅓ cup) vegetable oil
2 onions, finely chopped
2 tablespoons ginger and
    garlic paste
4 green cardamom pods, bruised
    and seeds removed
4 cloves
2 cinnamon sticks
2 teaspoons ground cumin
2 teaspoons ground coriander
1½ teaspoons ground turmeric
1 teaspoon chilli powder
½ teaspoon black mustard seeds
¼ teaspoon freshly ground
    black pepper
3 fresh or dried bay leaves
1 kg (2 lb 3 oz) beef chuck steak or
    other stewing beef, trimmed, cut
    into 3 cm (1¼ in) pieces
1 teaspoon sugar, or to taste
1 teaspoon sea salt, or to taste
Simple naan (see page 126), to
    serve

Heat the oil in a large frying pan or heavy-based saucepan over low heat. Add the onion and cook for 15 minutes, or until just golden and very soft. Add the ginger and garlic paste, spices and bay leaves. Add 125 ml (½ cup) of water and simmer until the water has almost evaporated.

Add the beef and 250 ml (1 cup) of water. Cover and cook for 45 minutes, then add another 125 ml (½ cup) of water and simmer, covered, for a further 45 minutes or until the beef is very tender (keep adding water if necessary to maintain a saucy consistency). Add the sugar and salt, to taste.

Serve with naan on the side.

Kerala Beef Curry

The people of Kerala love their beef curry. It doesn't matter which religion you belong to, if there was a competition for Kerala's favourite food, the beef fry would win hands down. Made using an aromatic spice blend, including fennel seeds, cinnamon and cardamom, this curry is made in every home.

80 ml (⅓ cup) coconut oil
2 red onions, thinly sliced
200 g (7 oz) tinned chopped
   tomatoes
100 g (3½ oz) shallots, chopped
135 g (5 oz) ginger and
   garlic paste
6 small green chillies, sliced
2 tablespoons ground coriander
1 tablespoon chilli powder
2 teaspoons ground turmeric
5 sprigs curry leaves, leaves
   stripped
1 kg (2 lb 3 oz) chuck steak or other
   stewing beef, cut into 2.5 cm
   (1 in) pieces
1 tablespoon vinegar
large handful of coriander (cilantro),
   roughly chopped
sea salt
Pilau (see page 124), to serve

Kerala-style garam masala
45 g (⅓ cup) fennel seeds
1 star anise, broken into pieces
1 cinnamon stick, broken into pieces
1 tablespoon cloves
2 teaspoons black peppercorns
2 teaspoons green cardamom pods
1 teaspoon freshly grated nutmeg

To make the Kerala-style garam masala, combine all of the spices except the nutmeg in a small dry frying pan over low heat and toast, stirring frequently, for 4–5 minutes, until lightly coloured and fragrant. Allow to cool slightly, then transfer to a spice grinder and blend to a coarse powder. Stir in the nutmeg. Store in an airtight container in the pantry for up to 3 months.

Heat the oil in a large heavy-based saucepan over medium heat. Add the onion and tomatoes and cook, stirring occasionally, for 10–12 minutes, until the onion is soft and the mixture is thick. Add the shallot, ginger and garlic paste and green chilli and cook for 8–10 minutes. Stir through the spices and 2 teaspoons of the Kerala-style garam masala, then reduce the heat to low and cook, stirring, for 1 minute. Add the curry leaves and cook for a further 3 minutes.

Add the beef, vinegar, coriander and 1 teaspoon of salt to the pan and stir well. Add 250 ml (1 cup) of water and stir again, then bring to the boil. Reduce the heat to low, cover and cook, stirring occasionally and adding a little extra water if the meat starts to stick to the base of the pan, for about 1½ hours, until the beef is tender. Season to taste.

Serve with pilau.

Lamb

Lamb Korma

There are many stories about the origins of korma. Some historians say it came with the Mughals when they invaded India from Persia. Other stories credit Rajput cooks for creating the dish in honour of the warrior Rajput 'Kurma' tribe. Whatever the truth, a korma is a delicious way to cook lamb and a real party pleaser.

3 tablespoons ghee

1 kg (2 lb 3 oz) boneless lamb
    shoulder, cut into 5 cm (2 in)
    pieces

sea salt and freshly ground
    black pepper

75 g (½ cup) raw cashew nuts

1 onion, roughly chopped

2 tablespoons ginger and
    garlic paste

1 cinnamon stick

1 tablespoon ground coriander

2 teaspoons ground cumin

1 teaspoon green cardamom
    pods, bruised

½ teaspoon Kashmiri chilli powder,
    or to taste

250 g (1 cup) natural yoghurt, plus
    extra to serve

Steamed basmati rice
    (see page 124), to serve

Heat 1 tablespoon of the ghee in a large heavy-based saucepan over high heat. Season the lamb well with salt and pepper then, working in batches, add to the pan and cook, turning frequently, for 5–7 minutes, until well browned. Transfer to a plate.

Meanwhile, process the cashews in a food processor until very finely chopped. Transfer to a bowl and set aside.

Add the onion and ginger and garlic paste to the processor and blitz until puréed.

Heat the remaining ghee in the pan over medium heat. Add the onion mixture and cook, stirring, for 10–15 minutes, until starting to caramelise. Increase the heat to medium–high, add the spices and cook, stirring constantly, for 3–4 minutes, until fragrant. Return the lamb to the pan along with the chopped cashew nuts, and stir to coat the lamb. Add just enough water to cover the meat, then season and bring to the boil. Reduce the heat to low and simmer, half-covered and stirring occasionally, for 1½–2 hours, until the lamb is very tender and the sauce is reduced to just cover the meat. Add a splash of water if the mixture starts to dry out.

Stir in the yoghurt and return to the boil, then reduce the heat and simmer over very low heat, uncovered, for 10–15 minutes, until the sauce is thick.

Serve with steamed basmati rice and extra yoghurt on the side.

Lamb Rogan Josh

A famed dish from the beautiful state of Kashmir, the fiery red colour of rogan josh comes from the chillies that are added in generous quantities. Rogan josh is usually cooked with tomatoes, but they are omitted here to allow the flavour of the lamb to shine through even more.

1 kg (2 lb 3 oz) boneless lamb shoulder or leg, cut into 2.5 cm (1 in) pieces
375 g (1½ cups) natural yoghurt
1 teaspoon sea salt
60 g (2 oz) ghee
1 cinnamon stick
2 teaspoons green cardamom pods, bruised
4 brown or black cardamom pods, bruised
½ teaspoon cloves
3 onions, chopped
2 tablespoons ginger and garlic paste
1 tablespoon Kashmiri chilli powder
2 teaspoons sweet paprika
2 teaspoons ground turmeric
large handful of coriander (cilantro), chopped
1 teaspoon garam masala
Paratha (see page 128), to serve

Combine the lamb, yoghurt and ½ teaspoon of the salt in a large bowl. Cover and set aside to marinate.

Heat the ghee in a heavy-based saucepan over medium heat. Add the cinnamon, cardamom pods and cloves and cook, stirring, for 30 seconds or until fragrant. Add the onion and remaining salt, reduce the heat to medium–low and cook, stirring occasionally, for 20–25 minutes, until golden brown. Add the ginger and garlic paste and cook, stirring, for about 30 seconds, until fragrant.

Add the lamb mixture, chilli powder, paprika and turmeric to the pan. Mix well and bring to the boil over medium heat. Reduce the heat to low and cook, covered, for 1¼–1½ hours, until the lamb is tender. Stir in the coriander and garam masala and season, to taste.

Serve with paratha on the side.

Saag Gosht

Even if you're not a fan of leafy greens, saag gosht is well worth making. Slow-cooking the lamb results in a very flavourful sauce that is quick to put together and utterly delicious.

1–2 tablespoons vegetable oil
1 kg (2 lb 3 oz) boneless lamb leg
    or shoulder, cut into 2.5 cm (1 in)
    pieces
sea salt
2 onions, finely chopped
1 cinnamon stick
1 large tomato, chopped or 200 g
    (7 oz) tinned chopped tomatoes
1½ tablespoons ginger and
    garlic paste
2 tablespoons mustard oil or
    vegetable oil
1 tablespoon ground coriander
2 teaspoons ground cumin
½ teaspoon ground turmeric
2 small green chillies, chopped
500 g (1 lb 2 oz) English spinach,
    washed and roughly chopped
½ teaspoon garam masala
Steamed basmati rice (see page
    124) or Chapattis (see page 131),
    to serve

Heat 1 tablespoon of the vegetable oil in a large heavy-based saucepan over high heat. Season the lamb with salt, then, working in batches, cook the lamb, turning frequently, for 5–7 minutes, until browned all over. Transfer to a plate.

Heat the remaining vegetable oil, if needed, in the pan over medium heat. Add the onion and cinnamon and cook, stirring, for 10–15 minutes, until starting to caramelise. Add the tomato and ginger and garlic paste and cook for 2 minutes or until the tomato is soft. Transfer to the plate with the lamb.

Increase the heat to medium–high and add the mustard oil. When the oil starts to smoke, reduce the heat to medium, add the ground coriander, cumin and turmeric and cook, stirring constantly, for 1–2 minutes, until fragrant. Return the lamb and onion mixture to the pan, along with chilli and stir to coat the lamb. Add just enough water to cover the meat, then season and bring to the boil. Reduce the heat to low and simmer, half-covered and stirring occasionally, for 1½–1¾ hours, until the lamb is tender and the sauce is reduced to just cover the meat. Stir in the spinach and return to the boil, then reduce the heat to low and simmer, uncovered, for 10–15 minutes, until the sauce is slightly thickened. Stir in the garam masala and season to taste.

Serve with steamed basmati rice or chapattis.

Lamb Dopiaza

This is a very comforting lamb dish where the meat is cooked in two stages: the first with onion and spices; and then with blended herbs and lemon juice, which further tenderises the meat. The herb mixture adds freshness to the dish and the results are mouthwatering.

1 kg (2 lb 3 oz) boneless lamb shoulder, cut into 5 cm (2 in) pieces
5 onions, thinly sliced
2 tablespoons ghee or vegetable oil
1½ tablespoons ginger and garlic paste
2 teaspoons sea salt
2 teaspoons Kashmiri chilli powder
1 teaspoon ground turmeric
½ teaspoon nigella seeds
30 g (½ well-packed cup) mint leaves
30 g (½ well-packed cup) coriander (cilantro) leaves
2 small green chillies, roughly chopped
½ teaspoon garam masala
lemon wedges, to serve
Pilau (see page 124), to serve

Combine the lamb, onion, ghee or oil, ginger and garlic paste, salt, chilli powder, turmeric, nigella seeds and enough water to barely cover the mixture in a large heavy-based saucepan. Bring to the boil over medium–high heat, then reduce the heat to low and simmer, covered, for 30 minutes. Remove the lid and cook for a further 1 hour or until the meat is tender and the sauce is thick.

Place the herbs, green chilli, garam masala and enough water to keep the mixture moving in a small food processor or blender and blend until smooth.

Add the herb mixture to the lamb mixture and cook, stirring, for a further 3 minutes. Season to taste.

Serve with lemon wedges and pilau on the side.

Kerala Lamb

This is a go-to entertaining dish in the state of Kerala as it's simple to make and the results are always impressive. To make things even easier, make the marinade the day before, then simply slow-cook the lamb and whip up some steamed rice before guests arrive.

1 kg (2 lb 3 oz) boneless lamb shoulder or other stewing lamb, cut into 4 cm (1½ in) pieces
1 tablespoon coconut oil
80 g (2¾ oz) thinly sliced fresh coconut
½ teaspoon black mustard seeds
2 sprigs curry leaves, leaves stripped
1 large onion, thinly sliced
2 long green chillies, sliced
3 cm (1¼ in) piece of ginger, julienned
3 garlic cloves, sliced
2 tomatoes, chopped
2 teaspoons sweet paprika
Steamed basmati rice (see page 124), to serve

Kerala lamb marinade
4 dried red chillies
2 cm (¾ in) cinnamon stick
1½ teaspoons coriander seeds
½ teaspoon cumin seeds
½ teaspoon fennel seeds
½ teaspoon black peppercorns
2 cloves
½ teaspoon ground turmeric
2 teaspoons ginger and garlic paste
1 long green chilli, sliced
2 teaspoons white vinegar

To make the kerala lamb marinade, roast the whole spices separately in a dry frying pan over medium heat for 30 seconds or until fragrant. Grind the toasted spices in a spice grinder or mortar and pestle to a fine powder, then transfer to a large bowl. Add the lamb and the remaining marinade ingredients and toss to combine, then cover and refrigerate for 2 hours or overnight.

Heat the oil in a large heavy-based frying pan over medium–high heat. Add the fresh coconut and cook, stirring, for 1–2 minutes, until lightly toasted. Transfer to a plate. Add the mustard seeds and curry leaves to the pan and sizzle for a few seconds, then add the onion, chilli, ginger and garlic. Reduce the heat to medium–low and cook, stirring occasionally, for 12–15 minutes, until the onion is golden. Add the tomato and paprika and cook for 8–10 minutes, until the tomato breaks down.

Add the lamb with its marinade to the tomato mixture. Stir well and add just enough water to cover. Bring to the boil, then reduce the heat to low. Add most of the toasted coconut (reserving some for garnish), then cover and cook, stirring occasionally, for 1½–2 hours, until the lamb is tender and the sauce has reduced and thickened slightly. If the mixture is still watery, remove the lid and continue to cook for a further 15–20 minutes.

Scatter with the reserved coconut and serve with steamed basmati rice.

Lamb Kofta Curry

Lamb koftas are a firm favourite as they're full of flavour and hold up well in robust sauces. You can make them ahead of time to make this dish even easier. They're delicious on their own served with a simple chutney for dipping, or served with naan for a more substantial meal.

2 tablespoons ghee or vegetable oil
1 onion, thinly sliced
1 tablespoon ginger and
    garlic paste
¼ teaspoon cumin seeds
400 g (14 oz) tin crushed tomatoes
1 teaspoon ground coriander
½ teaspoon chilli powder
1 teaspoon garam masala
250 ml (1 cup) coconut milk
    (see note)
Simple naan (see page 126), to
    serve
natural yoghurt, to serve

Lamb kofta
500 g (1 lb 2 oz) minced (ground)
    lamb
1 small onion, finely chopped
2 teaspoons ginger and garlic paste
½ teaspoon garam masala
25 g (⅓ cup) fresh breadcrumbs
large handful of mint leaves,
    chopped
large handful of coriander (cilantro)
    leaves, chopped, plus extra
    to serve
sea salt and black pepper

To make the lamb kofta, place the ingredients in a bowl and mix well. Using damp hands, roll tablespoons of the mixture into balls.

Heat a non-stick frying pan over medium heat. Add 1 tablespoon of the ghee or oil and, working in batches, cook the kofta, stirring gently, for 4–5 minutes, until lightly browned. Transfer to a plate.

Add the remaining ghee or oil to the pan along with the onion, ginger and garlic paste and cumin seeds, and cook for 4–5 minutes, until the onion is soft. Stir in the tomatoes, spices and coconut milk and bring to the boil. Reduce the heat and simmer gently for 5 minutes. Return the kofta to the pan and cook for a further 10 minutes or until the kofta are cooked through and the sauce has thickened slightly.

Scatter extra coriander over the top of the kofta and serve with naan and yoghurt on the side.

Note: If you prefer a slightly less rich sauce, use half coconut milk and half natural yoghurt.

Lamb Dhansak

When the Parsis (a Zoroastrian sect) escaped Arab persecution from Persia and landed on the shores of Gujarat in India, they brought with them their traditional recipes including dhansak. It was originally made with just meat but, once in India, the Parsis started adding lentils and vegetables, making it the comforting one-pot meal that's known today.

1 tablespoon ground coriander
1 teaspoon ground cumin
1 teaspoon ground cinnamon
½ teaspoon ground cardamom
½ teaspoon freshly ground
    black pepper
2 dried red chillies, soaked in hot
    water for 15 minutes, drained
4 long green chillies, chopped
handful of mint leaves, roughly
    chopped
handful of coriander (cilantro)
    leaves, roughly chopped
2 tablespoons ginger and
    garlic paste
1 teaspoon ground turmeric
1 tablespoon vegetable oil
600 g (1 lb 5 oz) boneless lamb
    shoulder, cut into 2 cm (¾ in)
    pieces
3 tablespoons ghee
3 onions, thickly sliced
1 large tomato, roughly chopped
160 g (⅔ cup) masoor dal (split red
    lentils), well rinsed
2 teaspoons tamarind purée
sea salt
Steamed basmati rice
    (see page 124), to serve

Roast the ground spices in a dry frying pan over medium heat for about 30 seconds, until fragrant.

Blend or process the drained chillies, green chilli, herbs, ginger and garlic paste, turmeric, roasted spices and oil until puréed.

Combine the lamb and spice purée in a large bowl. Cover and set aside in the fridge to marinate for at least 2 hours or overnight.

Heat the ghee in a large heavy-based saucepan over medium–high heat. Add the onion, then reduce the heat to medium and cook, stirring occasionally, for 12–15 minutes, until golden. Remove half the onion and set aside for garnish. Increase the heat to medium–high, then add the lamb and cook, stirring occasionally, for 8–10 minutes, until browned. Add the tomato and cook, stirring, for 2–3 minutes, then stir in the masoor dal and pour over enough water to cover.

Bring to the boil, then reduce the heat to low. Cover and cook, stirring often, for 1–1½ hours, until the lamb is tender (add extra boiling water along the way as the lentils cook and thicken the sauce). Stir in the tamarind purée and season with salt.

Reheat the reserved onion in a small saucepan and scatter on top of the curry. Serve with steamed basmati rice on the side.

Bhuna Gosht

Meat-based dishes in India are always sautéed in spices (a technique known as 'bhuna'), as it draws out the flavour of the meat, giving it a more robust texture and taste. You can substitute the lamb in this dish for chicken or beef; just remember to adjust the cooking time.

1 tablespoon coriander seeds

2 teaspoons cumin seeds

⅛ teaspoon black peppercorns

2 cm (¾ in) cinnamon stick

2 teaspoons fenugreek seeds

2 small dried red chillies

3 green cardamom pods, smashed and seeds removed

¼ teaspoon ground turmeric

1 large onion, roughly chopped

2 tablespoons ginger and garlic paste

1 long red chilli, roughly chopped

1 kg (2 lb 3 oz) boneless lamb shoulder, cut into 2.5 cm (1 in) pieces

60 g (¼ cup) natural yoghurt, plus extra to serve

3 tablespoons ghee, mustard oil or vegetable oil

400 g (14 oz) tin crushed tomatoes

½ teaspoon garam masala

coriander (cilantro) leaves, to serve

Chapattis (see page 131), to serve

Toast the coriander, cumin, peppercorns, cinnamon stick and fenugreek seeds separately in a dry frying pan over medium heat for 30 seconds or until fragrant. Transfer to a mortar and pestle or spice grinder, along with the dried chillies, cardamom seeds and turmeric and pound or grind to a fine powder.

Blend or process the onion, ginger and garlic paste and fresh chilli until puréed. Add a little water to get the mixture moving if needed.

Combine the lamb, yoghurt, onion mixture and spice powder in a large bowl. Cover and refrigerate for at least 2 hours.

Heat the ghee or oil in a heavy-based saucepan over medium–high heat. Add the lamb, along with the marinade and cook, stirring occasionally, for 3–4 minutes, until the lamb changes colour (be careful not to burn the spices). Add the tomatoes and enough water to come half way up the height of the lamb.

Bring to the boil, then reduce the heat to low. Cover and cook, stirring occasionally, for 1½ hours, until the lamb is tender. Remove the lid and continue to cook, uncovered, for a further 15–20 minutes, until the sauce has reduced and thickened enough to coat the lamb. Stir in the garam masala.

Scatter the curry with coriander leaves and serve with chapattis and extra yoghurt on the side.

Kashmiri Lamb Curry

The state of Kashmir may be known for its pristine beauty, but it's also famous for its complex cuisine, including flavourful meat-based dishes and a wide variety of breads and teas. This Kashmiri lamb curry is a staple in homes across the region, and it's also often made with goat. Any leftovers are delicious the next day, served with bread from the local bakery.

1 kg (2 lb 3 oz) boneless lamb shoulder or leg, chopped into 3–4 cm (1¼–1½ in) chunks
250 g (1 cup) natural yoghurt
1 tablespoon Kashmiri chilli powder
1 tablespoon ground coriander
1 tablespoon ground cumin
2 teaspoons ground turmeric
4 cm (1½ in) piece of ginger, finely grated
8 garlic cloves, finely chopped
60 ml (¼ cup) vegetable oil
2 red onions, thinly sliced
5 cloves
5 green cardamom pods
3 long green chillies, chopped
½ teaspoon ground fennel seeds
3 fresh bay leaves
400 g (14 oz) tin chopped tomatoes
2 teaspoons garam masala
sea salt
coriander (cilantro) leaves, to serve
Pilau (see page 124) or Paratha (see page 128), to serve

Combine the lamb, yoghurt, chilli powder, coriander, cumin, turmeric, ginger and garlic in a large bowl. Set aside in the fridge to marinate for at least 3 hours or, preferably, overnight.

Heat the oil in a large heavy-based saucepan over medium heat. Add the onion, cloves, cardamom, green chilli, ground fennel and bay leaves and cook, stirring occasionally, for 5 minutes or until the onion softens. Add the tomatoes and simmer for 2–3 minutes, until the oil starts to separate a little. Increase the heat and add the lamb, along with its marinade. Stir, allowing the lamb to lightly brown, then pour 250 ml (1 cup) of water into the pan. Cover and simmer gently for 35–40 minutes, until the lamb is tender. You can add more water if the sauce starts to dry out. Stir through the garam masala and season to taste with salt.

Scatter the curry with coriander leaves and serve with pilau or paratha on the side.

Basics

Steamed Basmati Rice

400 g (2 cups) basmati rice, rinsed

Place the rice and 750 ml (3 cups) of water in a heavy-based saucepan. Bring to the boil over high heat, cover and reduce the heat to low. Cook for 10 minutes then, without lifting the lid, remove from the heat and stand for a further 10 minutes for the rice to steam and finish cooking.

Gently separate the grains with a fork and serve.

Pilau

2 tablespoons ghee
3 Asian shallots, thinly sliced
1 sprig curry leaves, leaves
    stripped
2 garlic cloves, crushed
4 green cardamom pods, bruised
1 cinnamon stick
large pinch of saffron threads
400 g (2 cups) basmati rice,
    rinsed
800 ml (27 fl oz) chicken stock
    or water

Heat the ghee in a large heavy-based saucepan over medium–high heat. Add the shallot and cook, stirring, for 4–5 minutes, until golden. Add the curry leaves, garlic, cardamom, cinnamon and saffron and stir for about 1 minute, until fragrant. Add the rice and stir until well combined, then add the chicken stock or water and bring to a simmer, stirring occasionally. Cover with a lid, reduce the heat to low and cook for 10 minutes. Turn off the heat and stand, without removing the lid, for 10 minutes.

Alternatively, preheat the oven to 160°C (320°F) fan-forced. Melt the ghee in a large heavy-based flameproof casserole dish (Dutch oven) over medium heat, then add the shallot and cook until golden. Stir through the spices until fragrant, then add the rice and stir until well combined. Add the stock or water and bring to the boil, then cover and cook in the oven for 15–20 minutes, until the rice is tender.

Remove the whole spices, fluff gently with a fork and serve.

Simple Naan

A leavened, pillowy Indian-style flatbread, naan is traditionally made in tandoors or clay ovens, but it is possible to replicate this delicious bread at home in a very hot oven or even a frying pan. There is something delightful about dunking a hot piece of buttery naan into a rich curry and mopping up the sauce.

90 g (⅓ cup) natural yoghurt
1½ teaspoons instant dried yeast
450 g (3 cups) plain (all-purpose)
    flour, plus extra for dusting
1 teaspoon sea salt
½ teaspoon baking powder
60 ml (¼ cup) melted ghee, plus
    extra for brushing
½ teaspoon nigella seeds

Mix the yoghurt and 250 ml (1 cup) of warm water in a large bowl. Stir in the yeast, then add the flour, salt, baking powder and ghee. Mix with your hands to form a soft, sticky dough. Cover and set aside for 20 minutes.

Turn the dough out onto a floured work surface and knead for 1–2 minutes, until quite smooth. Cover and set aside in a warm place for 2–3 hours, until nearly doubled in size.

Preheat the oven to 250°C (480°F). Place two baking trays in the oven to heat up. Gently place the dough (without deflating it) on a well-floured work surface. Cut the dough into six wedges. With floured hands, gently pat and stretch each wedge into a 15 cm (6 in) circle, keeping them thin in the centre and thicker around the edge. Gently brush with ghee, then pull one side of each dough circle outwards or downwards to form the classic naan teardrop shape.

Carefully transfer the naan to the hot trays and bake for 6–7 minutes, until golden brown in spots and cooked through.

Serve immediately brushed with a little more ghee and sprinkled with the nigella seeds.

Note: For garlic naan, warm a clove of crushed garlic with the extra melted ghee in a small saucepan before brushing over the naan.

Paratha

Parathas take less effort to make than naan bread and are more indulgent than simple chapattis. The dough is made with both wholemeal and plain flour, resulting in a delicious chewy texture that's incredibly moreish.

110 g (¾ cup) wholemeal (whole wheat) flour
110 g (¾ cup) plain (all-purpose) flour, plus extra for dusting
½ teaspoon sea salt
¼ teaspoon baking powder
1 tablespoon ghee, plus extra, melted, for brushing and cooking
½ teaspoon nigella seeds

Sift the flours, salt and baking powder into a bowl. Add the ghee and rub it in with your fingertips until the mixture resembles fine breadcrumbs. Make a well in the centre and add the nigella seeds and almost 125 ml (½ cup) of water. Mix until you have a soft dough, adding the remaining water if needed. Cover and rest for 10 minutes.

Turn the dough out onto a lightly floured work surface and knead for 1–2 minutes, until smooth. Divide the dough into eight equal-sized portions, then roll each portion into a ball. Cover with a clean damp tea towel and set aside to rest for 30 minutes.

On a lightly floured work surface, roll out a ball of dough into a thin 17 cm (6¾ in) circle. Brush lightly with melted ghee, then fold in half, brush with more ghee and fold again into quarters. Cover with a tea towel and repeat with the remaining dough, then roll each portion of dough into a triangle about 2 mm (⅛ in) thick.

Heat a large non-stick frying pan over medium heat. Working with one paratha at a time, brush the top with melted ghee and cook, ghee-side down, lightly pressing all over with a clean dry tea towel, for 1–2 minutes, until golden brown in spots. Brush the top with ghee, then flip over and cook for a further 30–60 seconds, until golden and cooked through. Stack the paratha on a plate and cover with a clean tea towel to keep warm before serving.

Chapattis

Chapattis are a traditional Indian bread that can be found in almost every Indian home. Made with wholemeal flour and unleavened, they are simple to make and taste best freshly made. The dough is kneaded before lunch and dinner, then rolled out and cooked on a hot griddle just before serving.

225 g (1½ cups) wholemeal (whole wheat) flour or atta flour, plus extra for dusting
½ teaspoon sea salt
1 tablespoon ghee
melted butter, to brush (optional)

Sift the flour and salt into a bowl. Add the ghee and rub it in with your fingertips until the mixture resembles fine breadcrumbs. Make a well in the centre and add almost 125 ml (½ cup) of lukewarm water. Mix until you have a firmish dough, adding the remaining water if needed. Cover and allow to rest for 10 minutes.

Turn the dough out onto a lightly floured work surface and knead for 1–2 minutes, until smooth. Divide the dough into eight equal-sized portions, then roll each portion into a ball. Place the dough in a single layer on a baking tray. Cover with plastic wrap and set aside to rest for 30 minutes, or for as long as overnight.

Working with one ball of dough at a time, roll the dough out on a lightly floured work surface into thin 16 cm (6¼ in) circles.

Heat a large non-stick frying pan over medium–high heat. Once the pan is smoking hot, add a chapatti and cook, lightly pressing the dough all over with a clean dry tea towel in a dabbing motion, for about 1 minute, or until the base is lightly browned in spots. Flip the chapatti over and cook for a further 30–60 seconds. Remove from the pan and brush with melted butter if you like. Transfer to a plate and cover with a clean tea towel. Repeat with the remaining dough.

Serve straight away, or reheat briefly in a warm frying pan just before serving.

Tandoori Curry Paste

MAKES ABOUT
200 G (7 OZ)

½ small onion, roughly chopped
4 garlic cloves
3 cm (1¼ in) piece of ginger,
    roughly chopped
1 tablespoon ground cumin
3 teaspoons ground coriander
1 teaspoon ground turmeric
1 teaspoon sweet paprika
½ teaspoon chilli powder
1 tablespoon freshly squeezed
    lemon juice
natural tandoori or red food colouring

Blend all of the ingredients except the food colouring in a blender or the small bowl of a food processor to make a purée. Add a little water to get the mixture moving, if necessary. Add enough food colouring to make the mixture a deep red colour, about ½ teaspoon.

Store the tandoori paste in an airtight container. Leftover paste will keep for up to 2 weeks in the fridge or 3 months in the freezer.

Vindaloo Curry Paste

MAKES ABOUT
180 G (6½ OZ)

3 dried red chillies
60 ml (¼ cup) coconut vinegar or
    white vinegar
1 tablespoon cumin seeds
1 tablespoon coriander seeds
1 teaspoon fenugreek seeds
½ teaspoon black peppercorns
2 cm (¾ in) cinnamon stick
5 cloves
3 green cardamom pods, bruised
    and seeds removed
6 garlic cloves, crushed
4 cm (1½ in) piece of ginger,
    roughly chopped
3 green chillies, chopped
    (deseeded if you prefer
    a milder curry)
2 tablespoons soft brown sugar
¼ teaspoon freshly ground nutmeg
½ teaspoon ground turmeric

Soak the chillies in the vinegar and set aside to soften.

Roast the whole spices except the cardamom seeds separately in a dry frying pan over medium heat for about 30 seconds each or until fragrant. Grind with the cardamom seeds in a spice grinder to a fine powder.

Blend or process the soaked chillies and vinegar, garlic, ginger, green chilli, sugar, nutmeg, turmeric and ground spices to a fine purée.

Keep in an airtight container in the fridge for up to 1 week or in the freezer for up to 3 months.

Index

A

Aloo curry 48
aloo, Saag 28

B

balti, Chicken 75
Beef Madras 97
Bengali beef curry 98
Bengali fish curry 67
Bhindi masala 46
Bhuna gosht 118
butter chicken, Classic 70

C

Chana dal 20
chana dal temper 20
Chana masala 17
Chapattis 131
Chettinad, Chicken 82
Chicken balti 75
Chicken Chettinad 82
Chicken dopiaza 84
Chicken jalfrezi 79
Chicken tikka masala 76
Classic butter chicken 70
curry pastes
    Tandoori curry paste 132
    Vindaloo curry paste 132

D

Dahi machi 60
dal
    Chana dal 20
    Dal makhani 12
    Dal tadka 14
    Moong dal 18
Dal makhani 12
Dal tadka 14
Dhaba-style chicken 86
Dhaba-style temper 86
dhansak, Lamb 117
dopiaza, Chicken 84
dopiaza, Lamb 110

E

Eggplant masala 26
erissery, Mathanga 42
erissery temper 42

G

Goan pork sausage curry 92
Goan-style prawn curry 58
Goan-style vegetable curry 39
gosht
    Bhuna gosht 118
    Saag gosht 109

H

Hyderabadi chicken 81

J

jalfrezi, Chicken 79

K

kadhi, Sindhi 32
Kashmiri lamb curry 121
Kerala beef curry 100
Kerala egg roast 31
Kerala lamb 112
Kerala lamb marinade 112
Kerala-style fish curry 57
Kerala-style garam masala 100
kofta
    Lamb kofta curry 114
    Malai kofta 45
korma, Lamb 104

L

Lamb dhansak 117
Lamb dopiaza 110
lamb kofta 114
Lamb kofta curry 114
Lamb korma 104
Lamb rogan josh 106

M

Madras, Beef 97
Malai kofta 45
Malai kofta sauce 45
marinade, Kerala lamb 112
masala
    Bhindi masala 46
    Chana masala 17
    Chicken tikka masala 76
    Eggplant masala 26
    Kerala-style garam masala 100
    Paneer butter masala 36
    sambar masala 50
    sorpotel masala 94
    Tikka masala 54
matar, Mushroom 35
Mathanga erissery 42
Moong dal 18
moong dal temper 18
Mushroom matar 35
Mussels in curry sauce 62

N

naan, Simple 126

P

Paneer butter masala 36
paneer, Saag 40
Papad ki sabzi 22
Paratha 128
pastes
    Tandoori curry paste 132
    Vindaloo curry paste 132
Pilau 124
Pork sorpotel 94
Pork vindaloo 91
Prawn malai 64

R

rice, Steamed basmati 124
rogan josh, Lamb 106

S

Saag aloo 28
Saag gosht 109
Saag paneer 40
Sambar 50
sambar masala 50
sambar temper 50
sauce, Malai kofta 45
Simple naan 126
Sindhi kadhi 32
sorpotel masala 94
sorpotel, Pork 94
Steamed basmati rice 124

T

tadka 14
Tandoori chicken 72
Tandoori curry paste 132
Tandoori fish
temper
    chana dal temper 20
    Dhaba-style temper 86
    erissery temper 42
    moong dal temper 18
    sambar temper 50
Tikka masala 54

V

Vindaloo curry paste 132
vindaloo, Pork 91

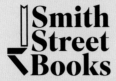

Published in 2022 by Smith Street Books
Naarm | Melbourne | Australia
smithstreetbooks.com

ISBN: 978-1-922417-58-9

All rights reserved. No part of this book may be reproduced
or transmitted by any person or entity, in any form or
means, electronic or mechanical, including photocopying,
recording, scanning or by any storage and retrieval system,
without the prior written permission of the publishers
and copyright holders.

Copyright text © Smith Street Books
Copyright design © Smith Street Books
Copyright photography © Emily Weaving

CIP data is available from the National Library of Australia.

Publisher: Paul McNally
Editor: Lucy Heaver, Tusk studio
Additional text: Bhavna Kalra
Designer: George Saad
Illustrator: George Saad
Typesetter: Heather Menzies, Studio 31 Graphics
Food photographer: Emily Weaving
Food stylist: Deborah Kaloper
Food preparation: Caroline Griffiths, Josh Nicholson and Meryl Batlle
Proofreader: Ariana Klepac
Indexer: Helena Holmgren

Printed & bound in China by C&C Offset Printing Co., Ltd.

Book 194
10 9 8 7 6 5 4 3 2 1